CHURCHES OF ESSEX

JOHN E. VIGAR

AMBERLEY

Front cover image courtesy of Simon Knott.

This edition first published 2025

Amberley Publishing
The Hill, Stroud
Gloucestershire GL5 4EP

www.amberley-books.com

British Library Cataloguing in Publication Data.
A catalogue record for this book is available from the British Library.

ISBN 978 1 3981 2301 4 (print)
ISBN 978 1 3981 2302 1 (ebook)

Typesetting by SJmagic DESIGN SERVICES, India.
Printed in Great Britain.

EU GPSR Authorised Representative
Appointed EU Representative: Easy Access System Europe Oü, 16879218
Address: Mustamäe tee 50, 10621, Tallinn, Estonia
Contact Details: gpsr.requests@easproject.com, +358 40 500 3575

CONTENTS

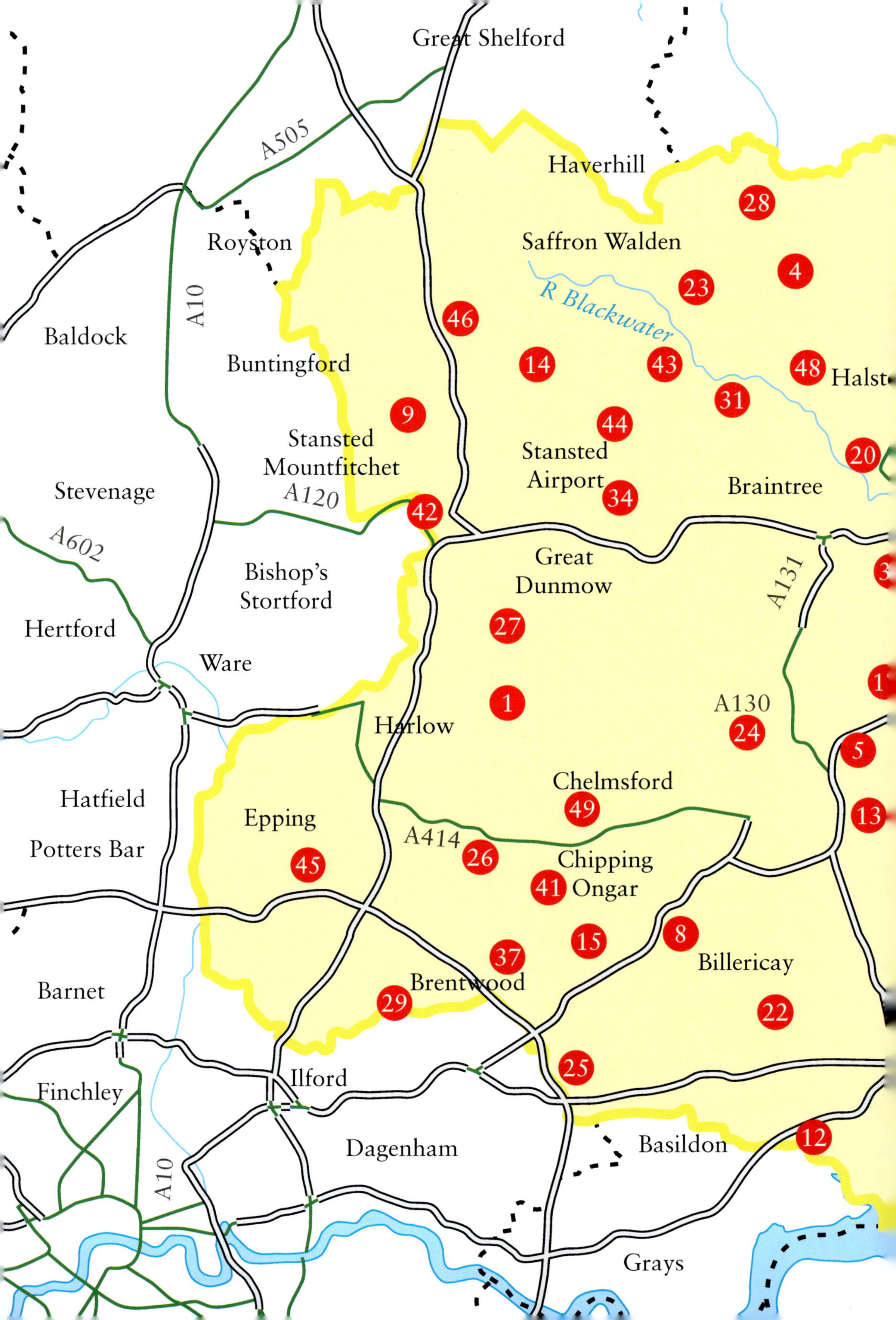

Great Shelford
A505
Haverhill
Royston
Saffron Walden
28
4
23
R Blackwater
Baldock
A10
46
14
43
48
Halst
Buntingford
31
9
44
20
Stansted
Mountfitchet
Stansted
Airport
Braintree
Stevenage
A120
34
42
A602
Great
Dunmow
Bishop's
Stortford
A131
Hertford
27
Ware
1
A130
Harlow
24
5
Hatfield
Chelmsford
Epping
49
13
Potters Bar
A414
26
45
Chipping
41
Ongar
15
8
37
Billericay
Brentwood
Barnet
29
22
Ilford
25
Finchley
Dagenham
Basildon
12
A10
Grays

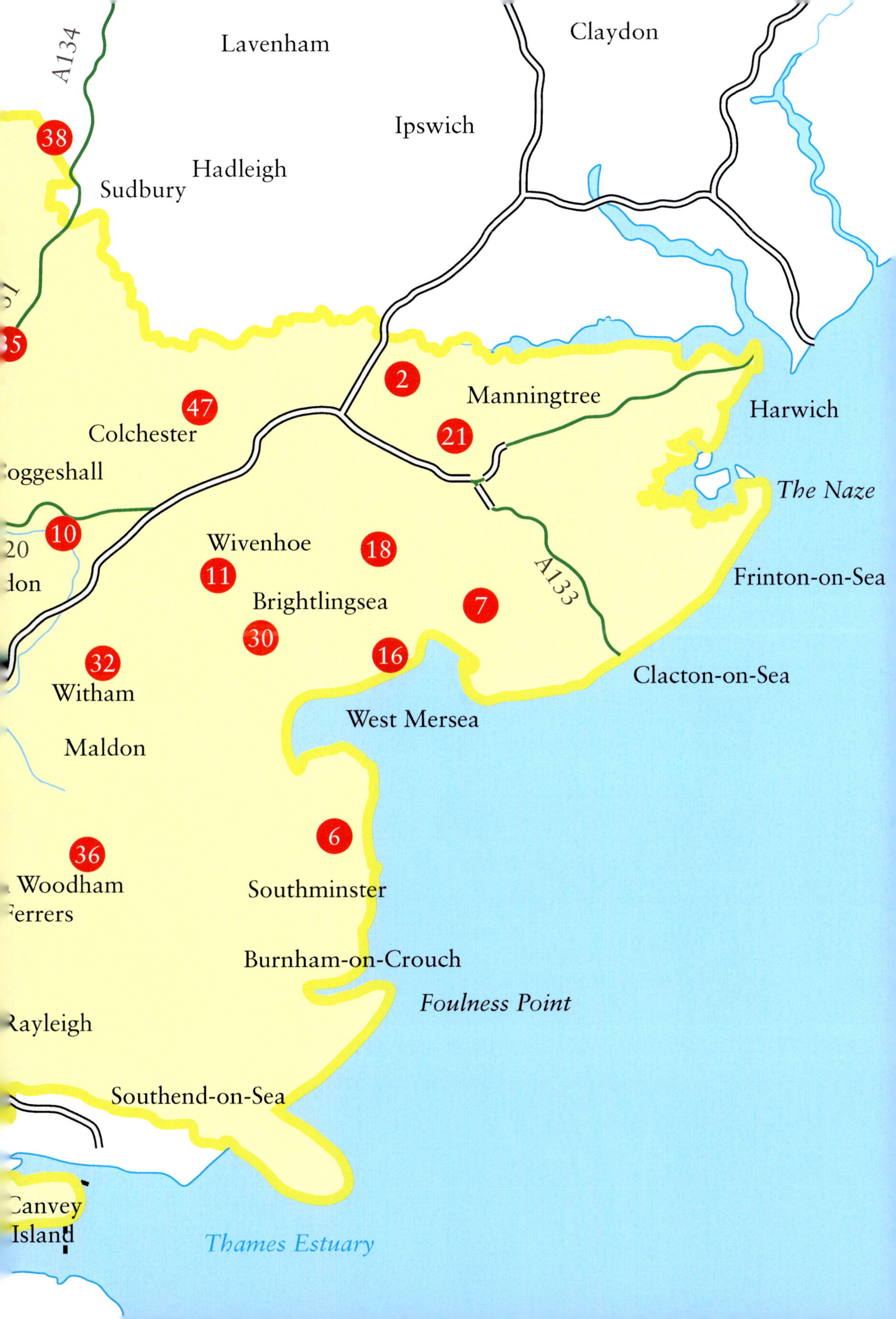
A134
Lavenham
Claydon
Ipswich
Hadleigh
Sudbury
38
35
47
Colchester
oggeshall
2
Manningtree
21
Harwich
The Naze
10
20
don
Wivenhoe
11
18
Brightlingsea
7
A133
Frinton-on-Sea
30
16
32
Witham
Clacton-on-Sea
West Mersea
Maldon
6
36
Woodham
Ferrers
Southminster
Burnham-on-Crouch
Foulness Point
Rayleigh
Southend-on-Sea
Canvey
Island
Thames Estuary

Introduction

Sandwiched between two counties that are known for their interesting churches, Suffolk and Kent, it is little wonder that Essex can boast many important religious buildings. Yet in comparison they are little known, even to church aficionados. In part this is due to the inaccessibility of some, but also because Essex as a county has been much maligned. A county that boasts many churches of Saxon origin, the oldest timber-framed church in the country and one of the best Arts and Crafts churches in Europe deserves to be better known and, in this book, I want to share the wealth of religious architecture both humble and grandiose that I think is worthy of greater exploration. Essex churches are often plain and simple, but even in the most isolated locations medieval wealth, particularly of the Norman period, has left us with huge, impressive buildings, unparalleled even in adjacent counties. Several parish churches were originally home to a monastic community, though this doesn't necessarily mean that they were grand structures. One former monastery, Waltham Abbey, can boast of the tomb of a king of England. Flint and timber are the usual building materials encountered, supplemented by the use of brick, particularly in the Tudor period when it was frequently used with panache to construct huge towers. Architecture apart, the furnishings of Essex churches can be in a league of their own. In common with other eastern counties, Essex has a large range of monumental brasses and its proximity to London means that its churches also contain magnificent monuments to families with city connections. Those links, which continue today, often meant that money was plentiful in the nineteenth century and few Essex churches escaped wholesale improvements by the Victorians. In the twentieth century many churches were beautified by the gift of stained-glass windows, making Essex one of the best counties to study the medium. Here you will find churches both small and large, simple, and quirky, each one representing the tastes, finances, and lives of generations of Essex residents.

1. Abbess Roding, St Edmund

Unlike many Essex churches there is no Norman architecture to see here, although its dedication to St Edmund suggests an early church must have existed. That assumption is further helped by the font, now held together by an iron band, which is certainly of the Norman period with one of its sides carved with two charming suns. The rest of the church is late medieval, of simple nave and chancel plan. Dividing the two is a late medieval rood screen which now has a Victorian crest. It is a shame it has been varnished so heavily. The pulpit has a magnificent sounding board with a marquetry star inset into its underside and next to it a wrought iron hourglass stand which once supported the parson's timepiece!

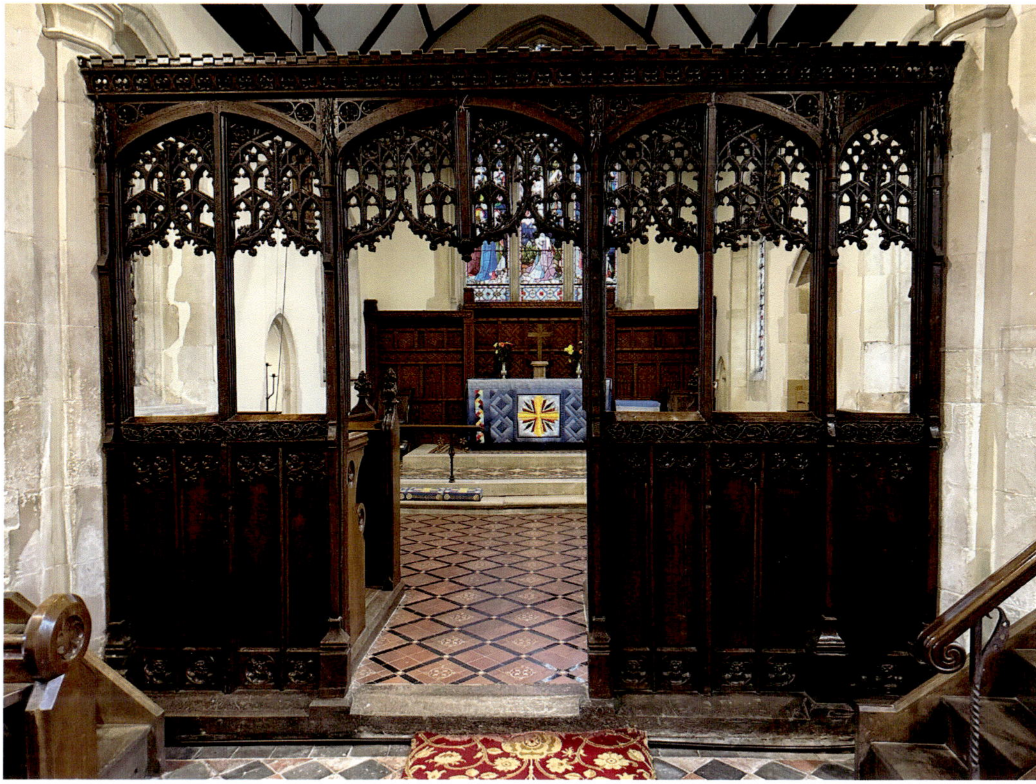

Abbess Roding showing the fifteenth-century rood screen. The cresting is modern and replaces the original rood loft.

The church contains two important early seventeenth-century monuments. On the north wall of the nave is an alabaster monument to Sir Gamaliel Capell (d. 1613), his wife and children which retains some of its original paint. The figures face each other across a prayer desk and their armorial bearings are displayed between green ribbons. This style of monument had been in favour for several decades. However, the monument opposite it, which is twenty years later, is something altogether different. It commemorates one of the daughters shown on the previous monument, Mildred Capell, Lady Luckyn, who is portrayed face on, her head resting on her right arm, and her left hand on a Bible. She sits beneath a canopy, the curtains of which are being pulled back by cherubs. Two more (acrobatic) cherubs offer her the crown of eternity. Mildred married William Luckyn who was created a baronet by Charles I in 1629. She sadly died five years later; her husband remarried and lived another forty years. Their son became an ancestor of the present Earl of Verulam, and the Capel family is still associated with the church. Mildred would certainly have recognised some of the stained glass now collected in the south chancel window which is made up of medieval fragments recovered from other windows in the church. They include a well-preserved bishop.

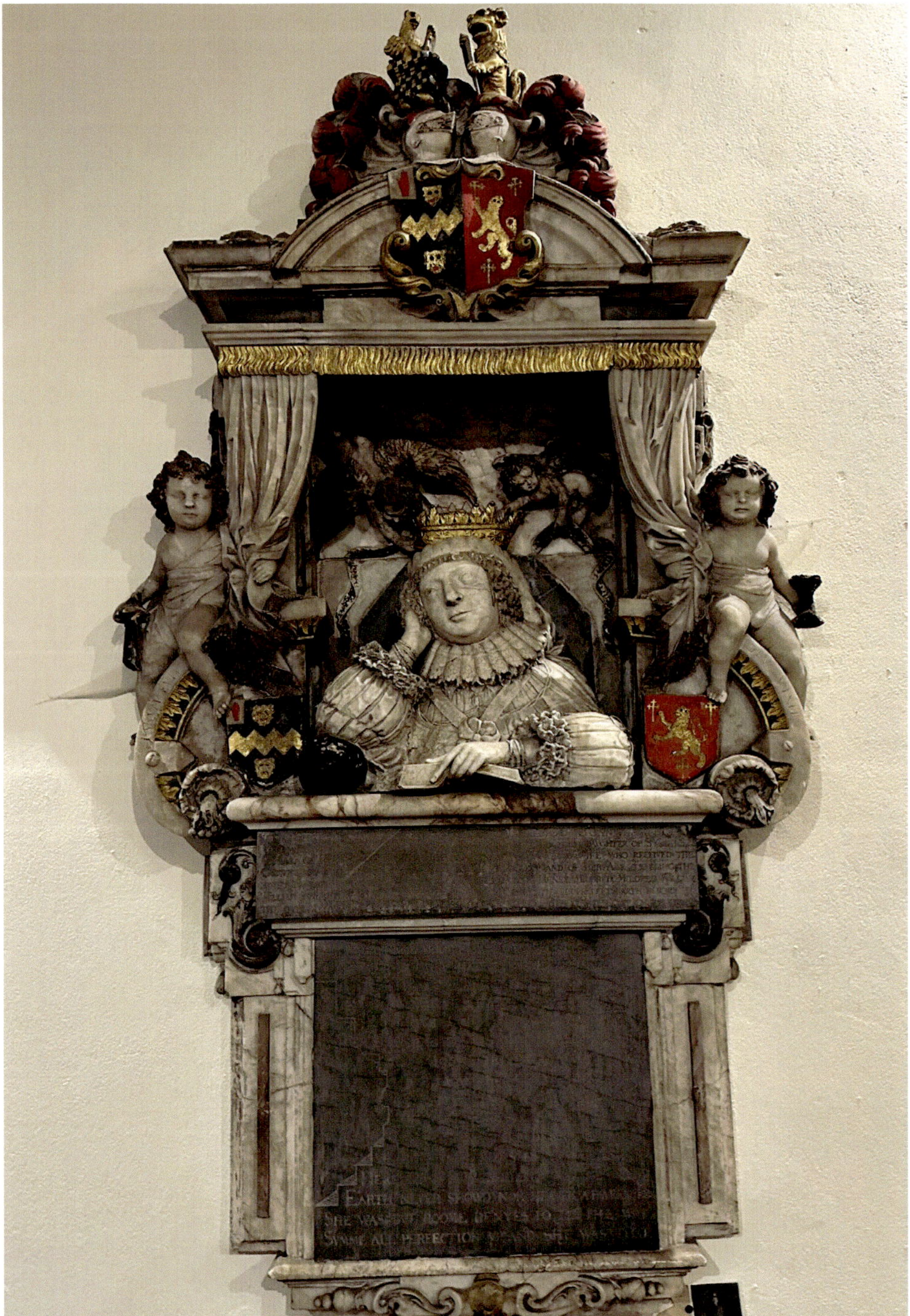

Abbess Roding. The monument to Lady Luckyn where cherubs hold back the curtains to reveal her portrait bust.

2. Ardleigh, St Mary the Virgin

What an extraordinary church this is, at the centre of its village and much loved by the wider community. The medieval tower is unlike any other in the county. Its base is constructed of flint flushwork but above that is made of dark brown puddingstone, or conglomerate, which is found in the gravel beds. Unlike most medieval churches whose outer walls were plastered over, this must have been left visible, so proud they were of being 'different'. The parapet returns to flushwork, but this time set into brick. The porch is an extraordinary example of flint flushwork with two delicious lions as label stops and St Michael and the dragon in the spandrels (see 18. Fingringhoe for a similar design). The three image niches are nineteenth-century replacements. The rest of the church is a rebuild of 1882, the medieval structure being in poor repair, but the work was carried out by William Butterfield (1814–1900), which means that it is far from pedestrian! It is the chancel that we have really come to see, where there is not a plain area of floor, walls or ceiling. The decoration followed a decade after the completion of the rebuild and was inspired by the Essex priest cum architect Fr Ernest Geldart (see 32. Little Braxted). The sanctuary is the most elaborately decorated part with grape vines to symbolise Holy Communion, images of the Four Evangelists and

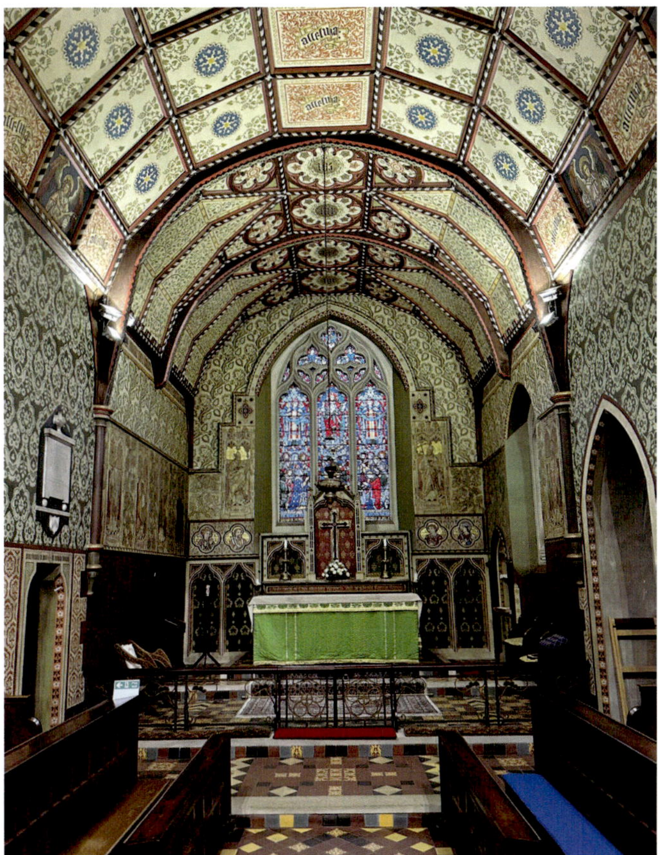

Ardleigh showing the rich nineteenth-century decoration of the chancel, much of which was designed by Revd Ernest Geldart.

of seven early saints. The east window by Bell and Beckham, who also painted the rood over the chancel arch in the nave, depicts the Risen Christ with the Twelve Apostles. The reredos has a shelf into which is built a plain cross, as putting a standing cross and candlesticks on the Holy Table was frowned on at the time, and this was a good compromise. In the south chapel Butterfield rescued a fifteenth-century image niche from the old church. It now houses a 2004 limewood statue of Our Lady and Child by Sara Wilkinson. The base of the fifteenth-century rood screen also survives and repays detailed inspection as the spandrels of the panels contain tiny carvings of heads and at least one dragon. As you leave, high in the porch is an unusual wooden memorial to Mr and Mrs Henry Lufkin dating from the early eighteenth century. Thomas Lufkin took his fellow villager Richard Large to court 100 years earlier for calling him 'a base rogue, shag-hair'd rogue, blockheadly rogue, and a bastard'.

3. Belchamp Walter, St Mary

Sitting on a bend of a lane overlooked by the chocolate-box Belchamp Hall, this is a much-visited church, and rightly so, for it contains many rare treasures. Much of the building is fourteenth century, including the south door, pitted with iron nails which displayed legal notices over the centuries. The tower is 100 years later and stands on a decorative flint plinth which leads one to suspect that it was planned on a grand scale, that plan only being resurrected with the matching battlements some generations later. On the exterior north side of the church is a rare insurance fire mark more commonly found on domestic buildings. Before the days of a national fire service it would tell the local firemen that the church was insured by the Royal Insurance Company (formed 1845) and act as an advertisement for them. Inside the church the visitor is attracted at once to the fine series of wall paintings which were painted just after the church was built. Some scenes are easy to identify, particularly the death of St Edmund, the Last Supper and Our Lady breast-feeding the baby Jesus. Other images are not so well preserved. Also standing out is the tall chimney for a cast-iron 'Tortoise' stove. Look at the top of the stove where you'll see the Tortoise logo and the motto 'Slow but Sure Combustion'. These were once commonly found in our churches, but the majority have been destroyed as better forms of heating have been installed. On the north wall of the nave is a huge fourteenth-century tomb recess for Sir John de Boutetourt, who died in 1324. He was quite a character, having been Admiral of the Northern Seas and Governor of Framlingham Castle, serving under Edward I and Edward II. The monument has lost his effigy and all its original colour, but even so it is one of the finest of its date in England. A grand eighteenth-century monument in the chancel commemorates the Raymond family who built the current hall. The Victorian pulpit is of far higher interest than many as the Four Evangelists are painted by George Washington Brownlow (1835–76). As his Christian names suggest, he was born in the north-east of England, at Newcastle Upon Tyne, but came to live in Belchamp Walter in his thirties. He is best known for his genre paintings, but these images of Matthew, Mark, Luke and John are especially fine. Brownlow is buried in the churchyard and commemorated by the stained-glass window set into the back of the Boutetourt monument.

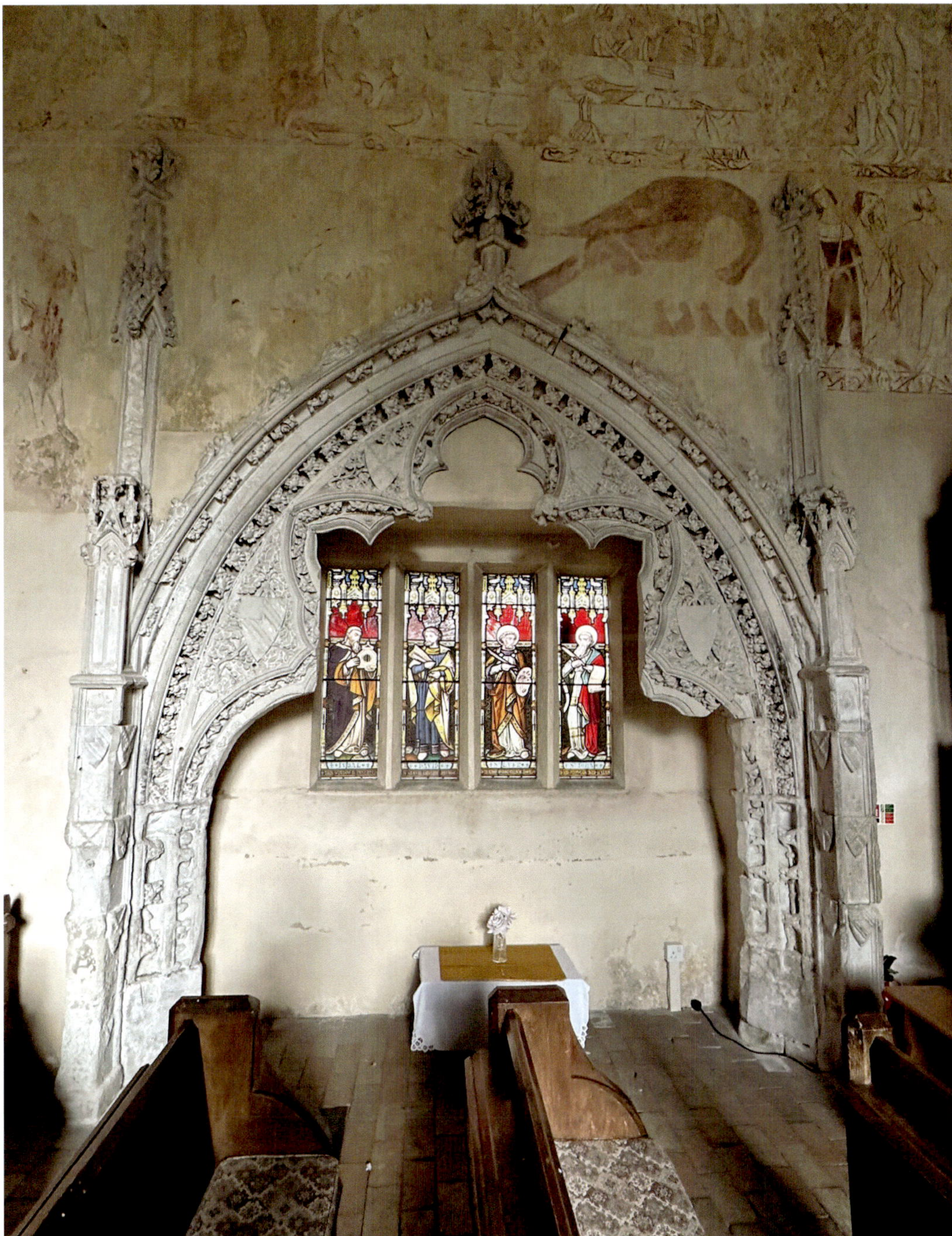

Belchamp Walter. This fourteenth-century tomb recess commemorates a member of the Boutetourt family and would originally have contained an effigy. Remnants of medieval wall painting can also be seen.

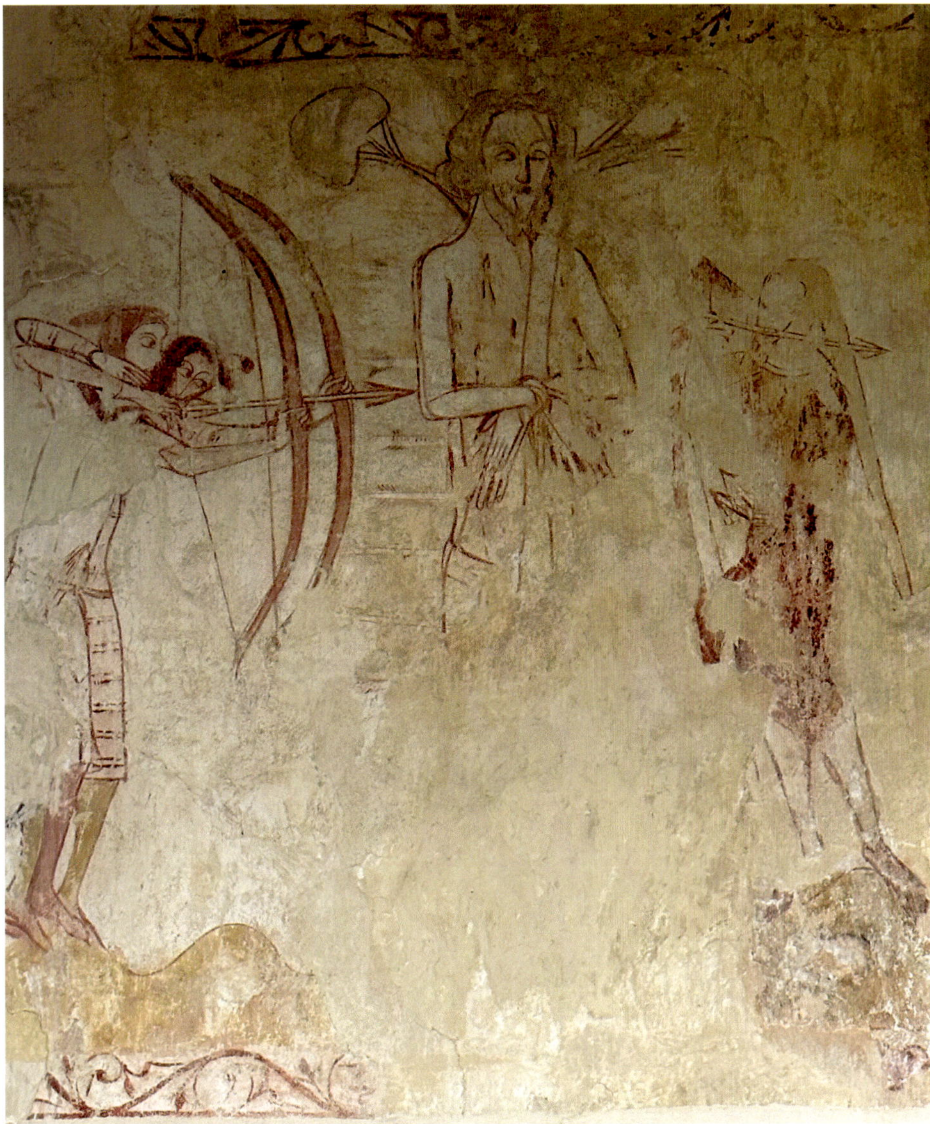

Belchamp Walter. This painting depicts the martyrdom of St Edmund of East Anglia, who was tied to a tree and shot through with arrows by Danish invaders. His four hands show how the original painting was later overpainted to make them larger.

4. Birdbrook, St Augustine of Canterbury

This is a simple Norman church which was thoroughly restored by the Victorians and then again in the 1960s creating a light, welcoming interior that shows off its interesting furnishings. As you go in don't miss the label stop showing Sir Winston Churchill in the porch! There is a good selection of memorials here. The most

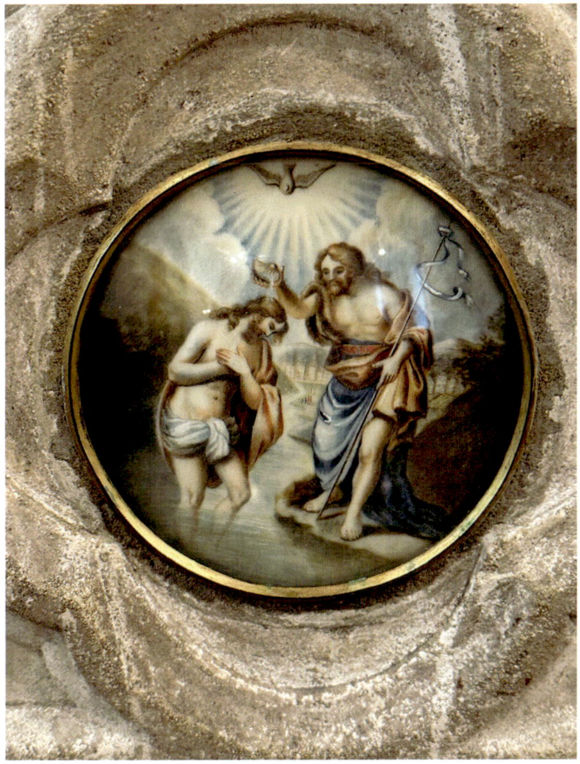

Right: Birdbrook. Set into the font is a porcelain plaque painted with an image of the baptism of Christ.

Below: Birdbrook. A memorial to the crew of a B17 bomber that crashed in the parish in 1944.

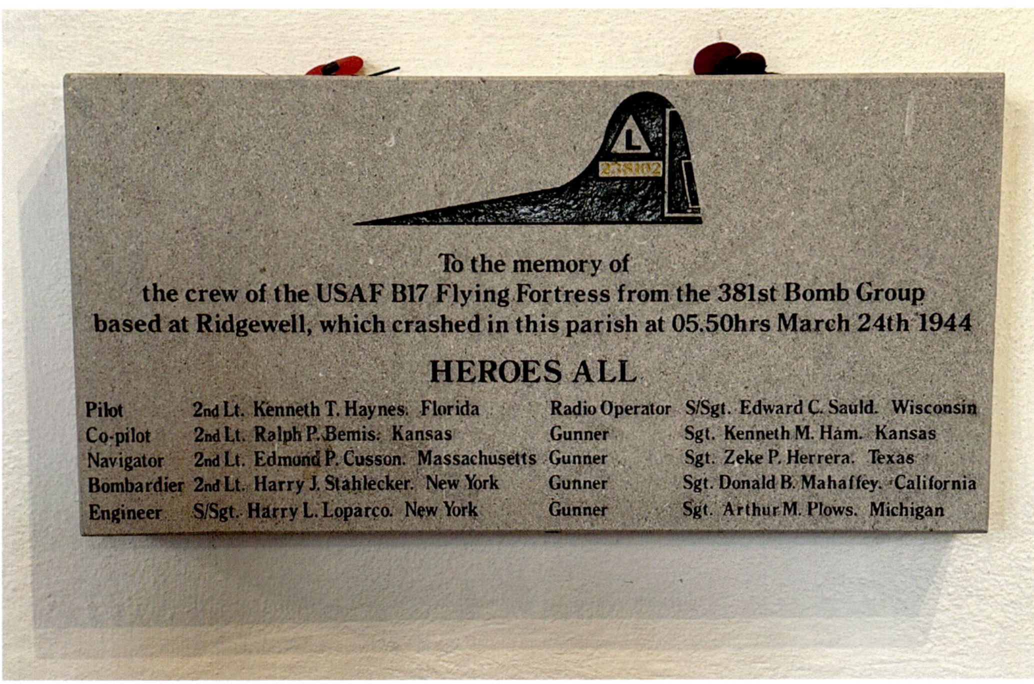

interesting, though not the most photogenic, may be found under the tower and commemorates Martha Blewitt (d. 1681) who had nine husbands! Thomas Walford (d. 1833) was a deputy lieutenant of Essex and a fellow of several academic societies. His tablet is framed by two extinguished torches, a popular nineteenth-century representation of death, and by a mourning female figure leaning against an urn. An earlier member of the family, James Walford, had a two-coloured marble tablet with a draped urn, but no female mourner. It is by the popular firm of King of Bath (see also 14. Debden) and also commemorates another Thomas who gave the present font to the church with its tiny painted panel showing the Baptism of Christ. However, the architecturally most important memorial here is to John Pyke (d. 1738) when it was the fashion to portray a sarcophagus. This stands underneath a triangular pediment which frames his shield of arms which, unsurprisingly, incorporates three fish! His will, written shortly before his death, requested that his coffin lid should not be fastened down until at least six days after his death, presumably to ensure that he wasn't buried alive (a common worry at the time). The church contains some very good examples of modern stained glass, the most recent of which is to the west of the door and is by Auravisions. It shows a rainbow, dove of peace and children playing. Most of the other windows are by Powell's and include some depicting former patrons of the church including the Saxon lord Ingua and his Norman successor FitzGilbert, Earl of Clare. The earlier one also shows the peasants building the church, whilst the latter depicts the Norman Conquest. Opposite, we find two later patrons: Walter of Wenlock, who was abbot of Westminster, and a Victorian master of Clare College, Cambridge. As part of the twentieth-century refurbishment the church was fitted with tasteful oak benches and panelling. On the south wall is a memorial to the ten members of crew of an American B17 bomber which crashed in the parish in 1944. Apparently, it was a brand-new plane full of bombs and had just taken off from Ridgewell Airfield 4 miles away when it encountered technical problems. Most of the crew were on their first mission.

5. Boreham, St Andrew

The first approach to this large, idiosyncratic church is memorable for a covered walkway which takes you from the pavement to the church porch. St Andrew's presents a real mixture of periods from Saxon (where Roman brick was extensively used) through Norman, thirteenth- and fourteenth-century enlargements to Tudor and early twentieth-century rebuilding. The oldest part of the church is the base of the tower, and inside the nave the tall blocked tower arch of Saxon date is clear to see. The nave was originally aisleless, the current arcades dating from the thirteenth century, having been cut through the original walls. Just inside the entrance door the original narrow aisle survives with a widely splayed lancet window in the west wall, but most of the aisle was later widened into a chapel-like space. Today it is the place to see many eighteenth- and nineteenth-century memorial tablets. Beneath the tower, mounted on the wall, are some medieval brasses. The inscription to Alice Byng (1573) tells us all about her illustrious husbands and shows her six children, who are all named, kneeling below. The chancel is long and tunnel-like and displays thirteenth-century wall paintings of the familiar red ashlar lines but also fragments

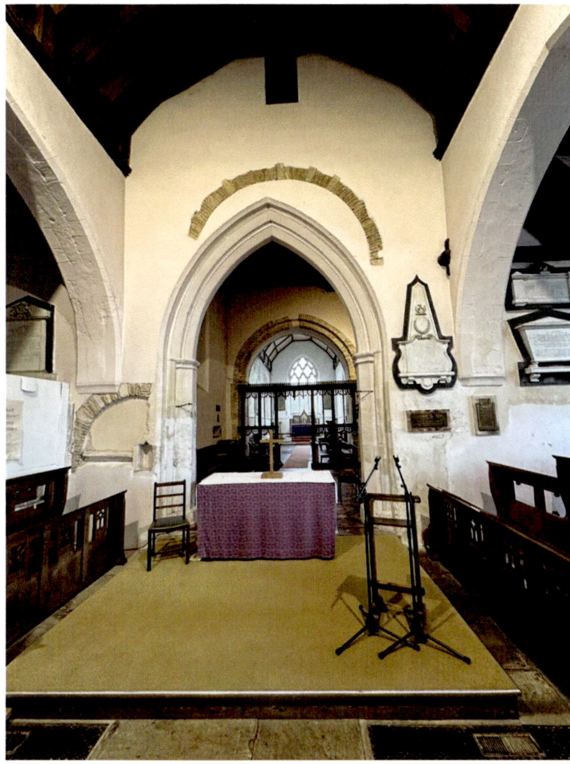

Right: Boreham. A view looking east in the nave showing the exposed brickwork of reused Roman bricks used by the Saxon builders.

Below: Boreham. The comical hat-wearing apes used at the feet of the first three earls of Sussex.

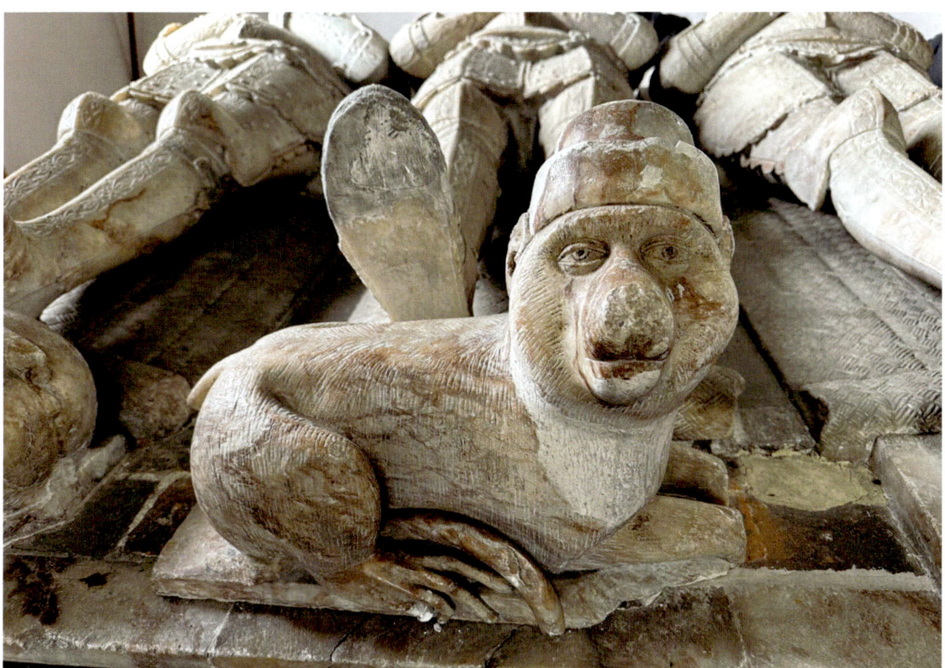

of what must have been a grand scheme of Victorian stencilling. To the south of the chancel is the Sussex Chapel, a Tudor structure erected to contain the magnificent tomb of the first three earls of Sussex. These men, members of the Radcliffe family, lived through politically charged times. Robert (1483–1542) rose quickly through the court of Henry VIII, even though his father had fallen from Tudor favour and had been executed. The 2nd Earl, his son Henry (1507–57), married into the powerful Howard family, and his son Thomas (1525–83) was appointed Lord Lieutenant of Ireland by Queen Mary. These three men had seven wives between them but are commemorated without them on a single tomb chest. It was carved in alabaster in London by Richard Stevens, who incorporated other rare stones in the construction. Unfortunately, it is now much damaged and the figures have had their hands sawn off and the heraldic bulls at their heads have mostly lost their heads, the damage probably occurring during the Commonwealth when any links with the Crown would have been frowned upon. All three men were Knights of the Garter, as can be seen on their effigies which, bizarrely, have apes at their feet, each wearing a jaunty hat!

6. Bradwell-on-Sea, St Peter on the Wall

The pilgrimage to this remote church is part of its charm. It stands on the site of a Roman fort called Othona, one of a series of forts constructed round the south-east coast of Britain and it was here in AD 653 that St Cedd landed from Lindisfarne to found a church. Cedd was a great church builder and is associated with the early history of several other English churches. The architecture of St Peter's is closely linked to a series of churches in Kent built at the same time, originally having a nave and apsidal chancel separated by a triple arcade

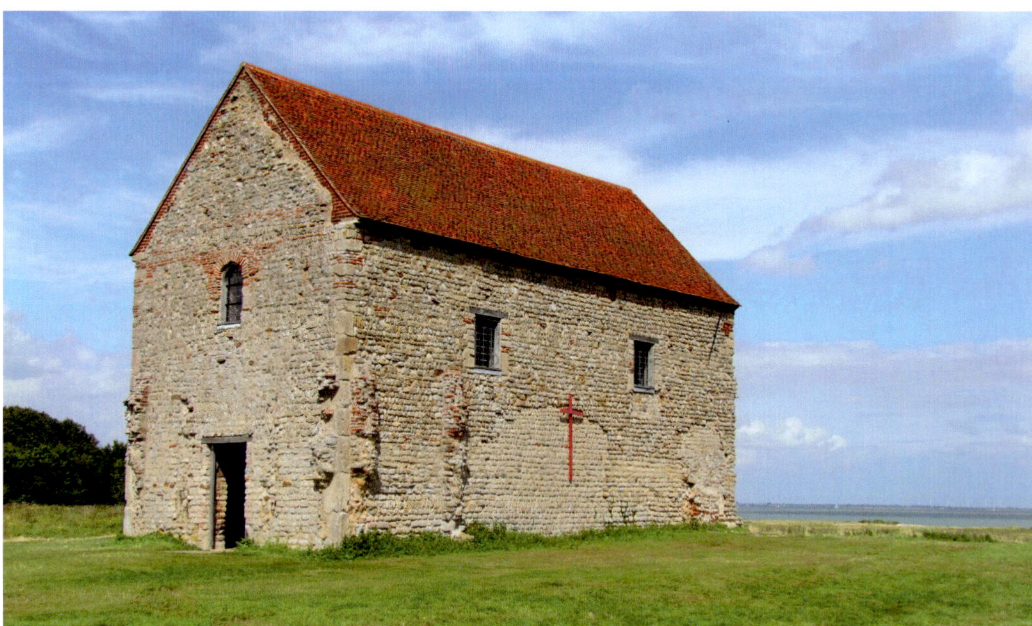

Bradwell-on-Sea. The chapel built by St Cedd in the seventh century. (Image by Simon Knott)

of arches. It also had individual burial chambers – or porticus – but these have disappeared together with the chancel, although their foundations are picked out in the grass. This is a plain barn-like church with little decoration, and it is all the more powerful for it. The tall walls are typical of the Saxon period and are partly built in materials reused from the Roman fort including brick and ragstone. Everywhere we can see rebuilding, blocked arches and repairs which we should expect in a building nearly 1,400 years old. During that time it has been the home of a monastic community, abandoned, used as a barn and only returned to use as a church in 1920. The interior is dominated by a large crucifix by Francis Stevens (1949), which has images of St Cedd, St Peter and St Paul on the arms of the cross and the Hand of God at the top. Beneath is a modern altar which incorporates stones from three other churches that were founded by St Cedd. If you look closely high on the east wall you can pick out the beginnings of the arches which would have originally separated the nave and chancel in the original church, whilst in the west wall an original window survives, constructed of reused Roman bricks.

7. Brightlingsea, All Saints

As one approaches from the north the sight of the fifteenth-century flint tower of All Saints' Church stands sentinel. A landmark to travellers by land and sea, this was once a thriving port and a member of the Cinque Ports Confederation. From the outside you could be forgiven for thinking that this is a late medieval church,

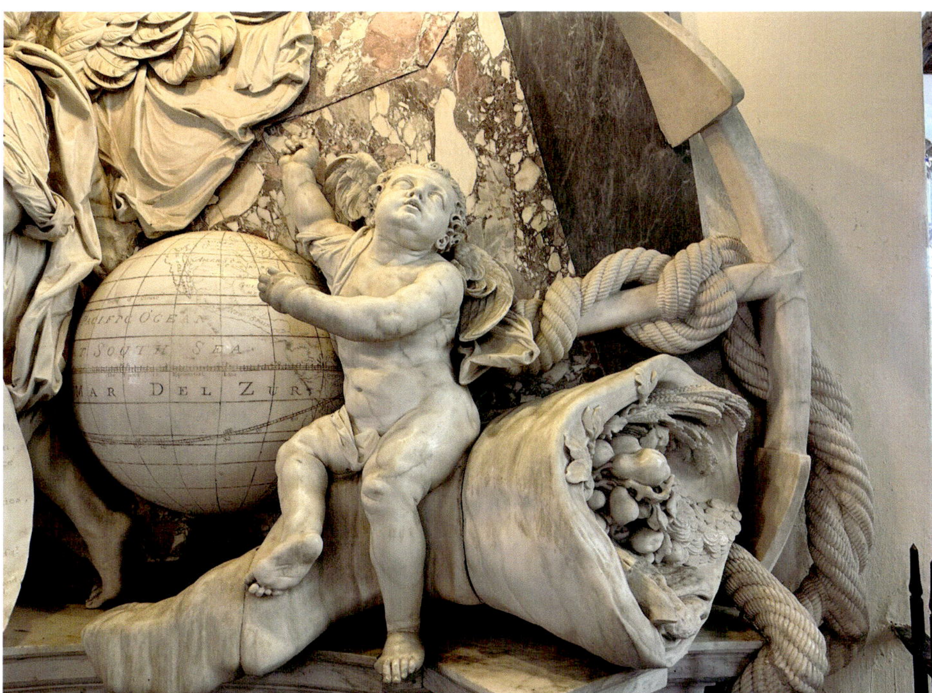

Brightlingsea. The huge Magens monument with geographical references which shows California as an island.

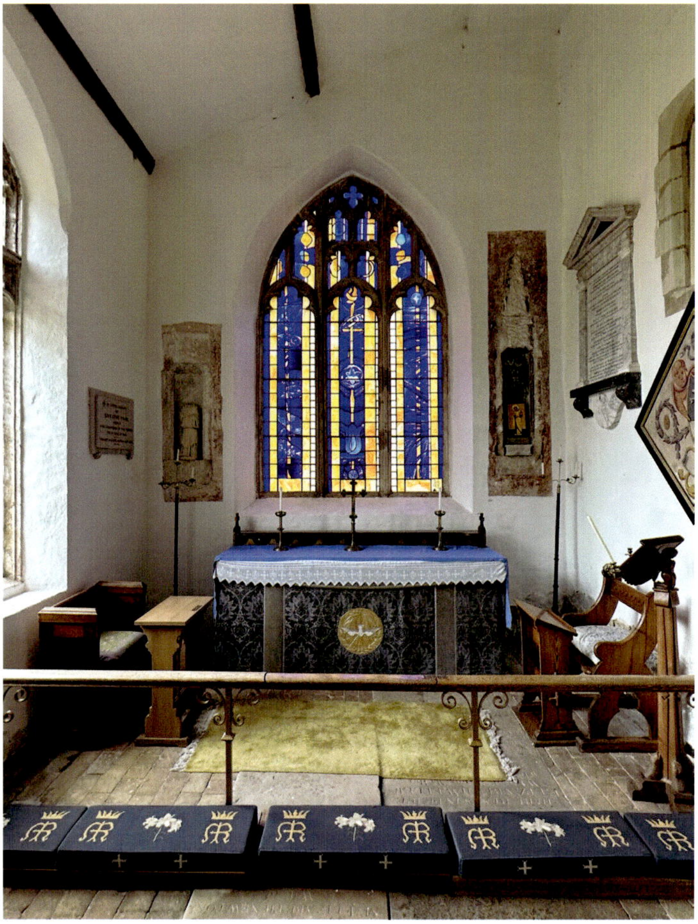

Brightlingsea. Interior of the north chapel with stained glass by Caroline Swash. Either side of the window are medieval image niches still with remains of their original colour.

but once inside it can be seen that at its core is a thirteenth-century building with fourteenth- to sixteenth-century additions. When the tower was finally built it was a separate building. This allowed its weight to settle before it was joined to the church – hence the change in arcade and blank area of wall at the west end. The nave roof fell when the medieval clerestory collapsed in the late Georgian period, so the roof dates from that period. I like the way the roof structure at the east end of the nave mirrors the chancel arch below. North and south chapels were added by medieval merchants at a time when saintly images were common so they both display multiple (now empty) niches that retain their original colour. That in the south chapel still has traces of a medieval painted inscription on its base. The north chapel floor contains important brasses to the Beriffe family, which include one displaying their merchant mark. The brasses to mother and daughter Alice and Margaret are reused memorials to fifteenth-century Augustinian canons, the brass having been turned over and a new picture cut. Margaret's long hair tells us that she was unmarried. The dramatic east window of the chapel was designed by Caroline Swash, whilst nearby is a fine modern statue of Our Lady by Essex sculptor John Doubleday. However, it is the chancel which contains the greatest surprise, the enormous marble monument to Nicholas Magens, a German merchant who was based in London in the eighteenth century. It was designed by little-known artist Nicholas Read who had worked under the famous French sculptor Louis-François Roubiliac. It shows a vast globe representing Magen's trading exploits – with California depicted as an island! A horn of plenty overflows with bounty, whilst above billowing clouds (for which Read is best known) burst out of their grey marble surround. Startingly, in the sanctuary life-size eighteenth-century cutouts of Moses and Aaron stand either side of the altar. Running around the walls of the aisles are a series of plaques, each of which records a Brightlingsea person who has died at sea since 1872. Each tells its own sad story and it is worth spending some time reading them all. The latest work of art to be installed in the church is an icon of St Catherine by Sallie Berriff, a direct descendant of the merchants who built the north chapel 500 years ago.

8. Buttsbury, St Mary

Only a mile from the bustling shops of Ingatestone High Street, but here you could be in another world, on high ground overlooking the valley of the embryonic River Widd. It is a medieval church in miniature with a weatherboarded porch and top to the brick west tower. The simple south door has an arch unrelieved of capitals – a feature that can also be seen in the nave arcades inside. This use

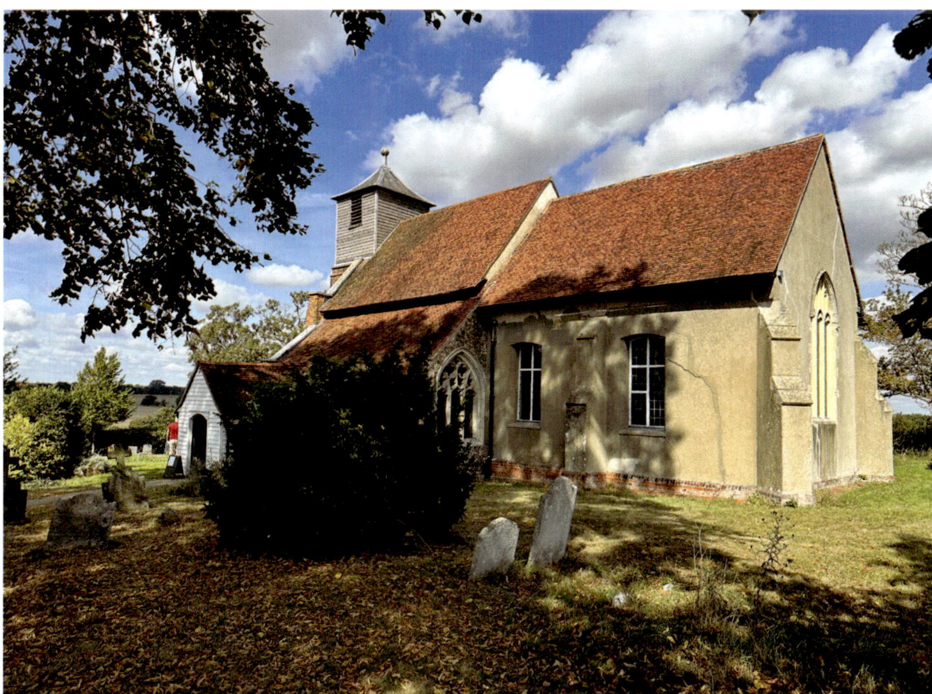

Buttsbury. Exterior from the south-east where we see the cement-rendered chancel, the huge window at the east end of the south aisle and the timber bell turret.

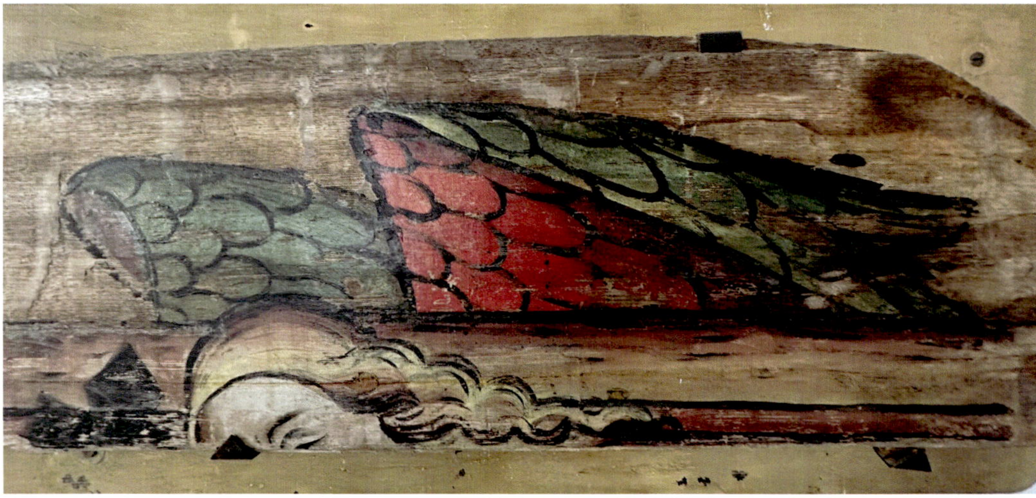

Buttsbury. This amazing fragment from the medieval rood was discovered hidden in the roof in 1977 and is now displayed in the chancel.

of pared-down Gothic was much copied by architects of the twentieth century. There is no chancel arch, which makes the church seem larger inside than out, the clear glass in the windows also helping in this regard. The east window is in the Perpendicular style and its stonework has been renewed, but the windows at the east end of both north and south aisles are Decorated in period and remain unrestored. They form quite a bravado display where little wall is left to support the roof above. When filled with coloured glass they must have looked even more stunning. In the nineteenth century the chancel was restored – see the tiled floor – but a lighter touch meant that the nave retains its slightly uneven brick floor with a prominent ledgerstone in the central gangway. The north door needs to be seen from the outside as it has ironwork in the form of the Scandinavian Midgard Serpent. Scientific dating has placed the door itself as late twelfth century and the ironwork can be compared to similar work at Eastwood church near Southend. In a very simple building, the First World War memorial forms an exotic flourish – this Gothic tablet was made by a parishioner and serves as both a roll of honour and a memorial to those killed. On the south wall of the chancel are displayed fragments of outstanding medieval art which formed part of the Doom painting which originally formed the division between nave and chancel. Here we see part of two angels and the halo of Christ. These were discovered in the roof in 1977, hidden behind plaster. The colours are as they would have been seen 500 years ago, with vivid reds and greens.

9. Clavering, St Mary and St Clement

This is a large, light, East Anglian-type church – quite an unusual find in this part of Essex – built below the village in the valley of the River Stort. The church itself is mostly late medieval and the thirteenth-century font of Purbeck marble (which must have been brought here via the river) would have been in the previous church on the site. In the south aisle is a delightful internal stair turret that takes the circular staircase to the rood loft, which originally stood above the screen. It even has a tiny window next to the chancel arch to give some light to the official charged with using it daily to keep the lamps and candle on top of the screen burning. Take a look at the staircase and you'll see how much the steps were worn away in the 200 years it was in use. On the left side of the doorway to the staircase there is a lovely piece of graffiti in Latin recording '*Amore Vincit Omnia*' or 'Loves Conquers All'. At first glance the rood screen, which dates from the fifteenth century, appears to be plain wood but when you get close you'll see that the outlines of paintings of saints survive. Again, this is a rare survival in Essex. With your torch it is much easier to see and you will be able to pick out the emblems of a few of the saints, although most are barely visible. When you look through the screen, you'll see just how plain the chancel is. It only contains one memorial, showing that for much of its history its patrons lived and were buried elsewhere, for it was only patrons and incumbents who could claim burial in the chancel. That is why the aisles of Clavering church are so rich in monuments. They are to prominent and wealthy local families who could not claim right of burial in the chancel. The earliest is the effigy in the north aisle of a thirteenth-century

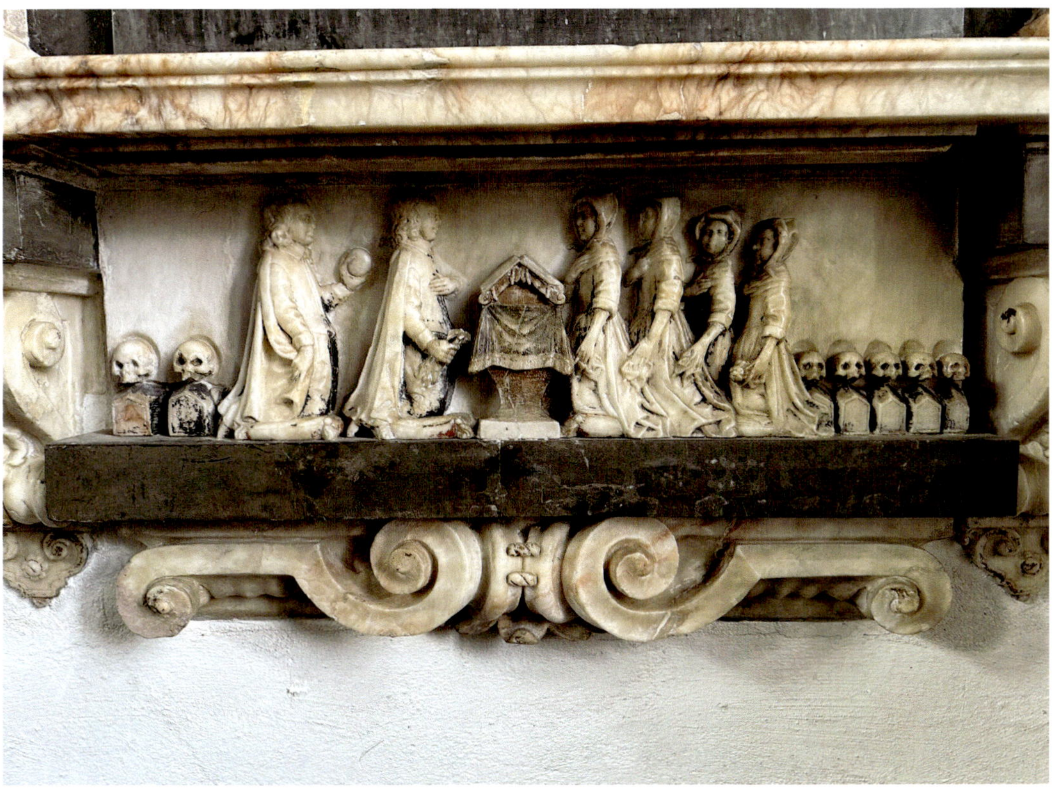

Clavering. At the base of one of the Barlee monuments the deceased children are represented by skulls sitting on top of their coffins. Of thirteen children, only six survived.

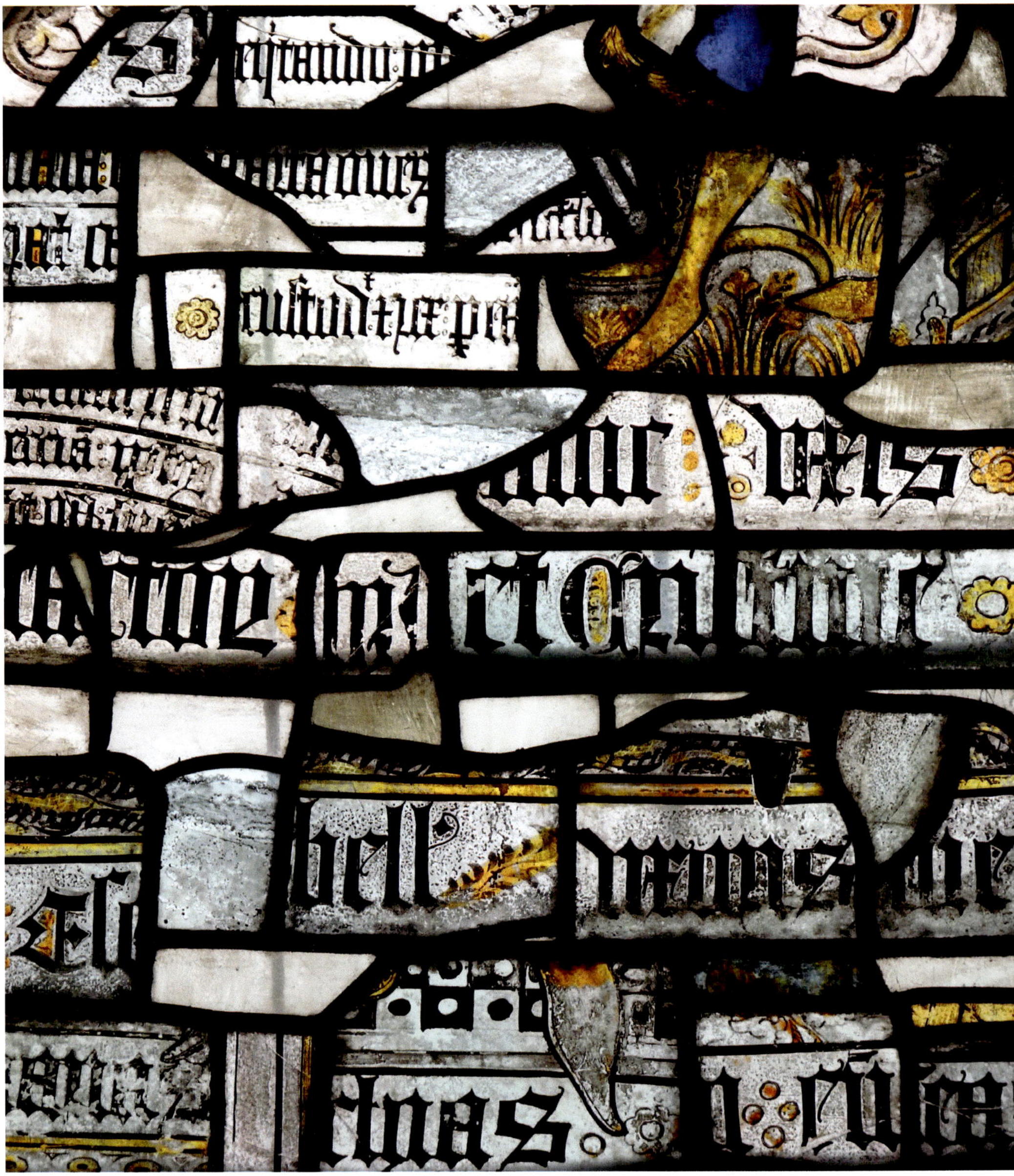

Clavering. The church contains a large collection of medieval glass fragments with this window predominantly being made up of fifteenth-century inscriptions.

knight, made of Purbeck marble just like the font. Sadly, there is no indication of who is commemorated. In the same aisle are a series of monuments to the Barlee family. Haynes Barlee (1606–96) is commemorated by a portrait bust shown as a young man with long hair rather than a bewigged nonagenarian. It is a historicising monument erected some fifty years after his death. His first two wives are depicted in grand monuments on the west wall. They are not quite identical but take a similar form. His first wife died at the age of thirty-six, having given him thirteen children who are depicted on the bottom of the monument. Sadly, only six survived her, the others each being represented by a skull on a coffin. His second wife was only married to him for just over two years and had no children but, as the inscription tells us, brought with her a 'considerable fortune'. The church contains a large amount of fragmentary medieval glass.

10. Coggeshall, St Peter ad Vincula

This huge church reminds us of the wealth created by the wool trade in the fourteenth century and of the individuals who profited from it. Sadly, the church suffered much damage in the Second World War, but the rebuilding by the architect Stephen Dykes Bower was an exemplary project and today the much-loved building is fit for another 500 years at least. From the exterior the nave, tower and porch are of local flints whilst the eastern end is constructed of Kentish ragstone blocks with brick crenelations. The vaulted porch contains a fine carving of the Pelican in her Piety which dates from the nineteenth century, and the upper room would have contained the church treasures. Once inside, the whole building

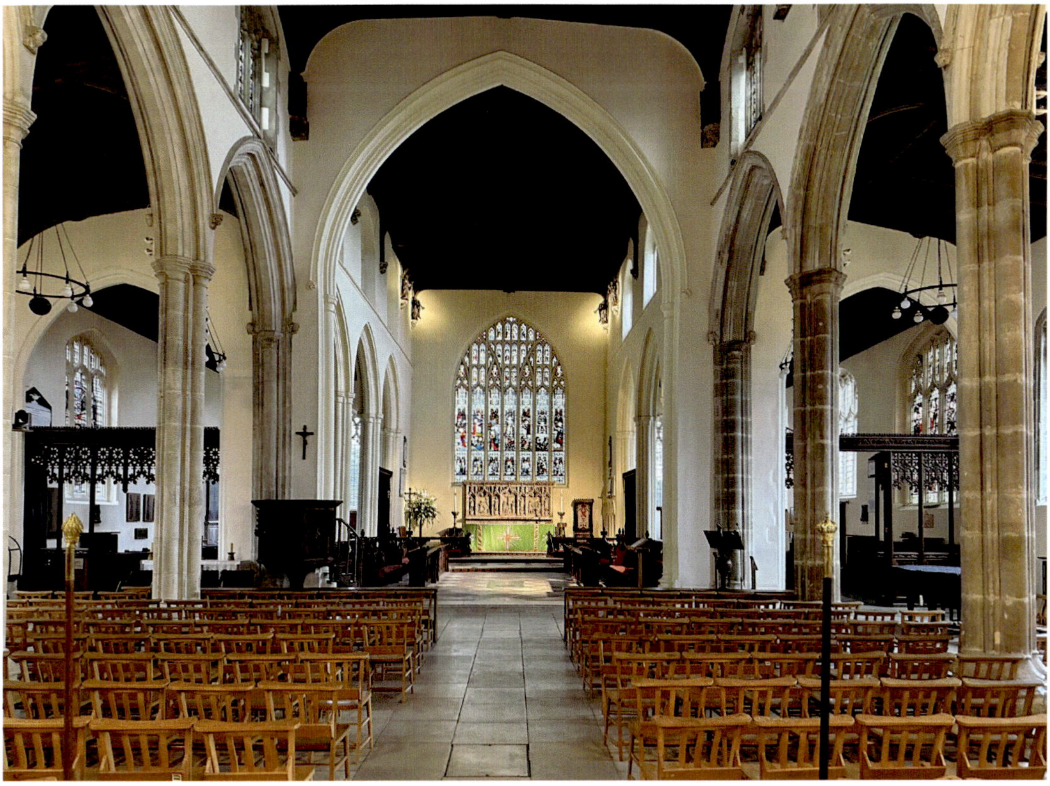

Coggeshall. The interior looking east shows the enormous proportions of this church built by wealthy late medieval clothiers.

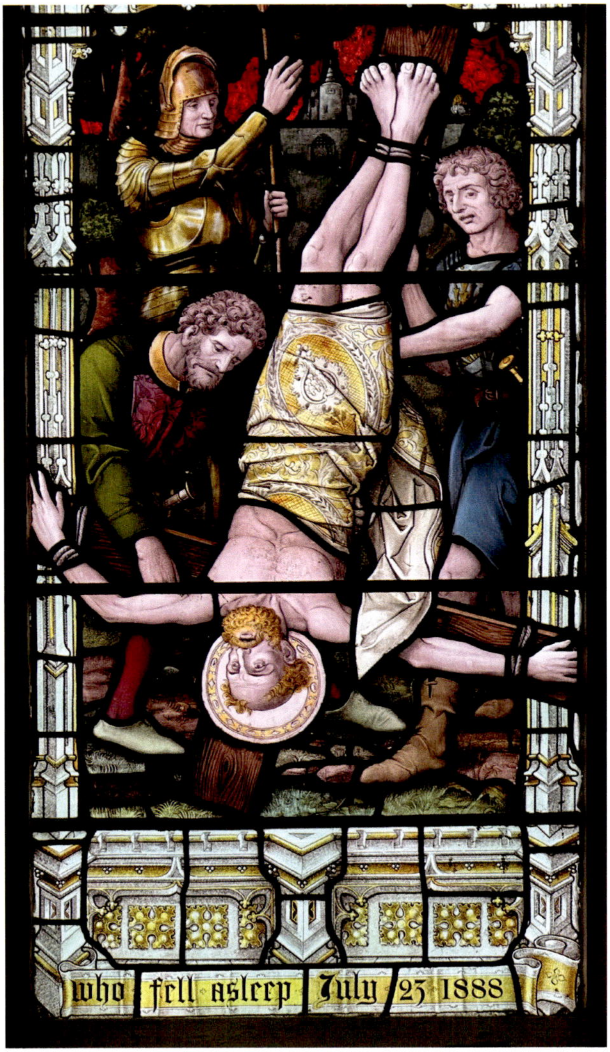

Coggeshall. The martyrdom of St Peter as depicted in an 1879 stained-glass window by Lavers and Westlake.

is visible through the enormous aisle arcades, which make the church seem even larger than it is. In the north chapel are the memorial brasses to some of the families whose wealth made this church possible, the Goldwyres and Paycockes. The former, represented by tall, thin brass effigies of husband and wife, is now mounted on the wall. He gazes out at us, but she looks past him in a disinterested way. Beneath them on the floor is the much grander brass to John and Joan Paycocke (1533) although their texts, inscriptions and an image of Our Lady have been lost and exist in outline only. Their house, now in the care of the National Trust, brings many visitors to Coggeshall through the summer. In the same chapel the east window is by the twentieth-century designer Leonard Evetts and depicts St Catherine (1974). Her famous wheel, which broke during her martyrdom, is clearly visible on either side. A more gruesome martyrdom is shown in the south chapel where a window by Lavers and Westlake (1879) shows scenes from the life of St Peter including his upside-down crucifixion. The chancel contains several monuments to the Skingley family, including one signed by Thomas Denman of London, and another with a very sad verse reminding us that death is never far away. In the floor are two brass plaques to mark the entrances to their vaults. My favourite monument in the church is in the south aisle and records the life of Robert Townsend who, whilst in his twenties, fought in the seven battles of the Wars of the Spanish Succession under the 1st Duke of Marlborough.

11. Copford, St Michael and All Angels

This is an unassuming church in the grounds of Copford Hall, slightly detached from its village. Yet here is a jewel house of medieval art. The church dates from the twelfth century and its elaborate decorative scheme of wall paintings is probably down to the bishops of London who owned the manor at the time. Furthermore, the church was originally stone vaulted and therefore of a much higher status than other Essex churches. Sadly, the vaulting was destroyed when the south aisle was added, taking many paintings with it, yet the lower series of images survives in a fragmentary state. The best paintings by far cover the apse, although they have been overpainted. We find Christ in Majesty attended by angels who hold the circular image for us to view, surrounded by the buildings of the New Jerusalem. Christ sits

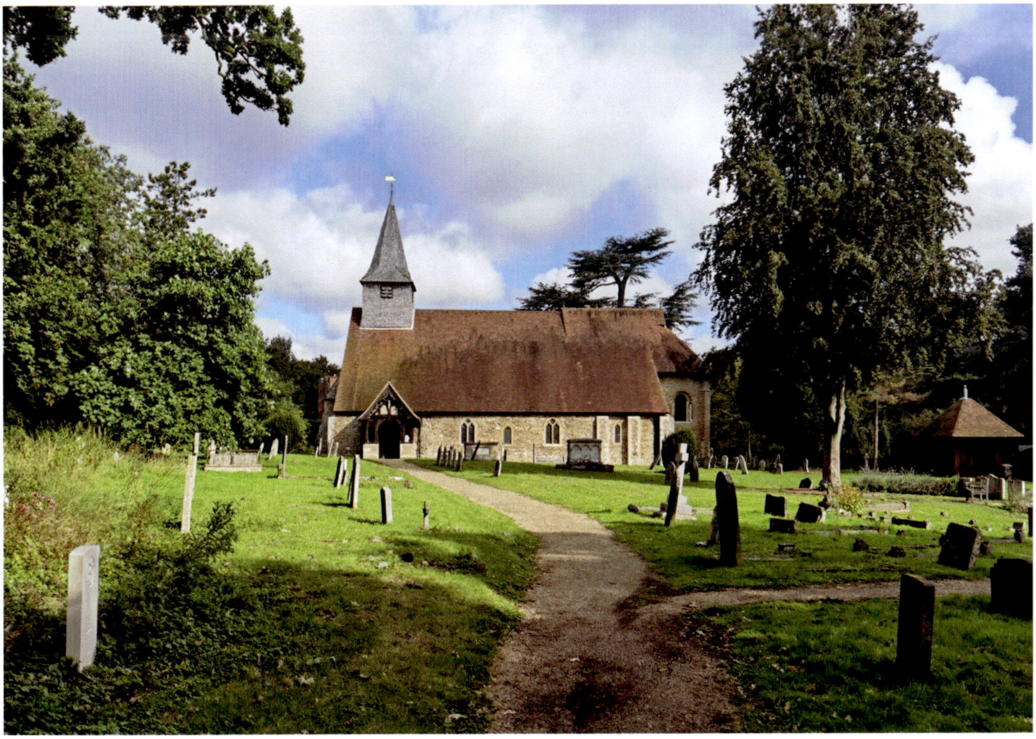

Copford viewed from the south. The nave and aisle have a catslide roof and it is possible to see the apsidal chancel on the right-hand side. (Image by Simon Knott)

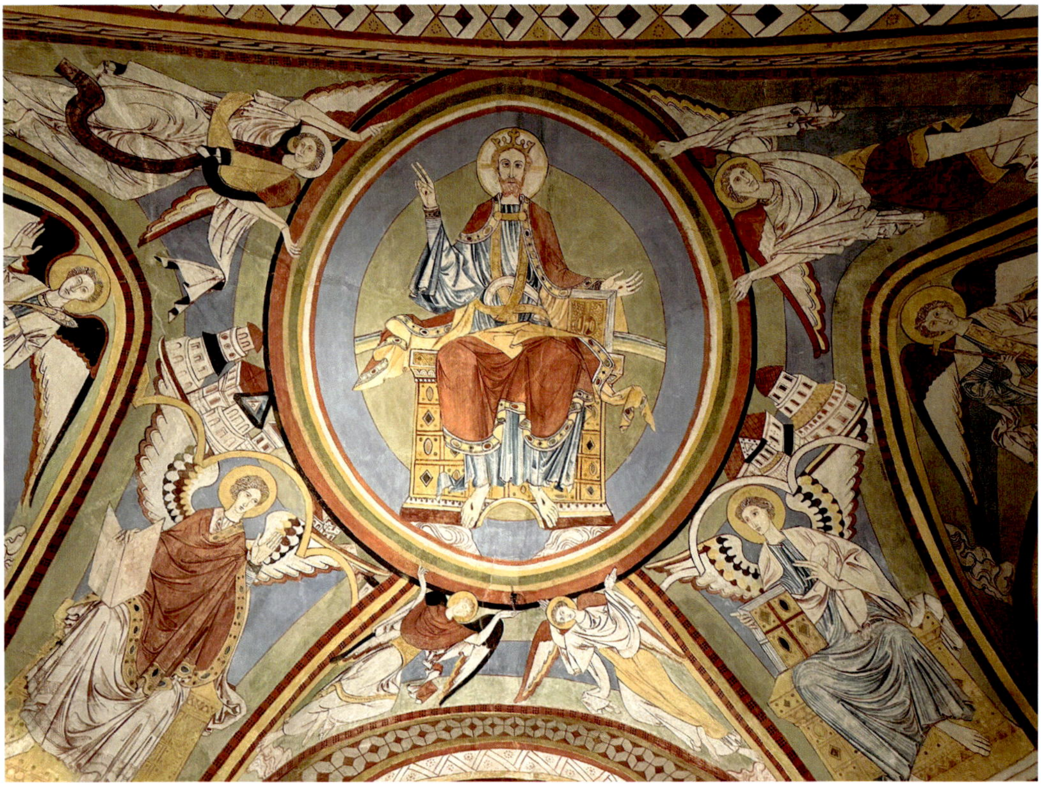

Copford. The church contains an early decorative scheme, although much has been overpainted. Here we see Christ in Majesty.

on a throne and displays his wounds, his right hand raised in blessing. It is interesting to compare the style of these twelfth-century paintings with the Victorian depictions of the Annunciation and the Adoration of the Shepherds, both by Clayton and Bell of 1886, that fit into the space within the gable above the arch. With the absence of a chancel arch the division between nave and chancel is formed by a fifteenth-century rood screen. Here there is much evidence of where the Romanesque vault once formed the division – its pilaster-like supports crudely chamfered off to open the building up. Decorative delights aside, the great treasure of Copford Church must be the brick arch between nave and south aisle. It soars up like those brick churches of the Baltic, a bravura composition in the then latest material. Some of the bricks are reused Roman (there are plenty more to be seen if you walk around the outside of the church), but the majority in this arch were purpose made, making them the earliest use of new brick construction in the county. The octagonal piers suggest a date in the middle of the Decorated style of architecture, which was fashionable from 1250 to 1350. To prove that our parish churches are the result of centuries of addition and alteration, the choir stalls, which date from the 1950s, are some of the finest of their date, with each bench end depicting a different animal. Look for a fox, rabbit, otter, hedgehog, squirrel and a koala!

12. Corringham, St Mary

This is a delightful spot – village-like – though you'll have to make prior arrangements to visit the church. The huge tower dates from the Norman period and is built of Kentish ragstone, brought by water from Maidstone, down the Medway and across the Thames. Its lower corners, or quoins, are formed of tufa, which is a limestone deposit much favoured by the Normans, who extracted it from the beds of chalk streams. It has the appearance of a white sponge. Another tell-tale sign of Norman work is the herringbone pattern of stones in the south chancel wall, where you can also see a vertical join where the original chancel ended until it was extended in the early thirteenth century to give more room for ceremonial introduced by the Fourth Lateran Council of 1215. The north aisle, which was added in the fourteenth century, has walls of striped alternating flint and ragstone which is a Thameside fashion we see in both Essex and Kent. This is a much-loved church the interior of which reflects its High Church tradition. The statue of Our Lady was designed by Martin Travers (1886–1948) a pupil of Sir Ninian Comper, who worked here in 1939. Dividing the north aisle from its chapel is a very early wooden screen with simple cusped tracery. On its eastern side is some intriguing seventeenth-century graffiti. The chapel still contains

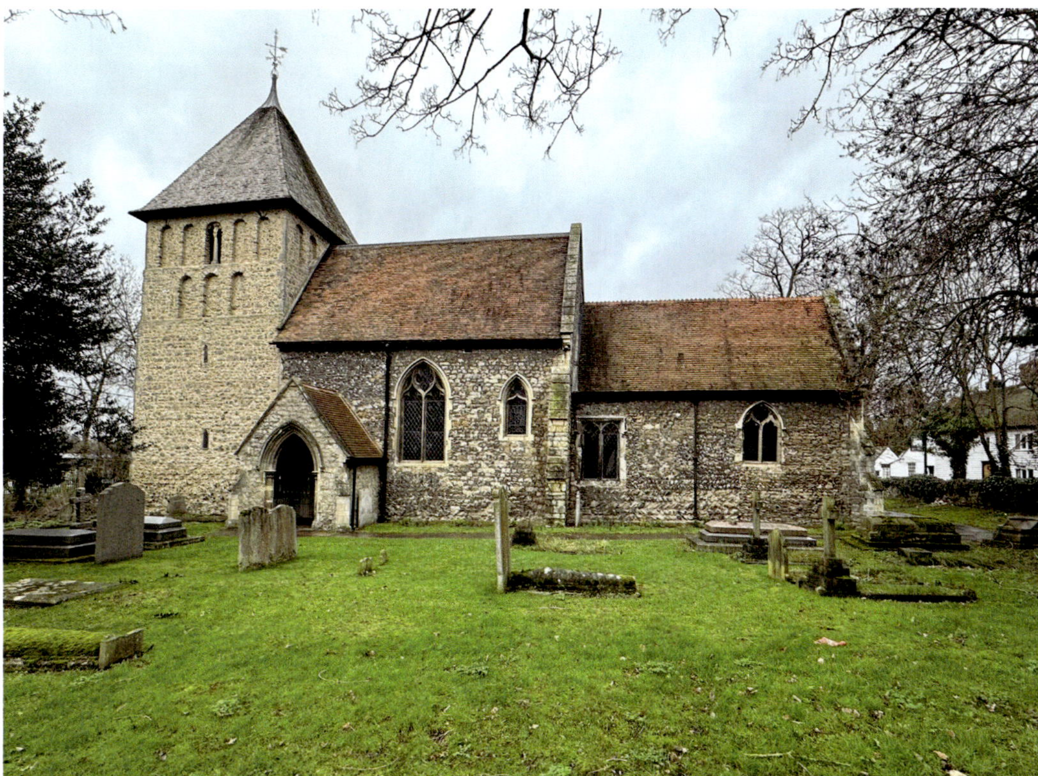

Corringham. Much of the church is Norman and built of Kentish ragstone. You can pick out the south wall of the chancel where the stones are laid in herringbone form in the lower levels.

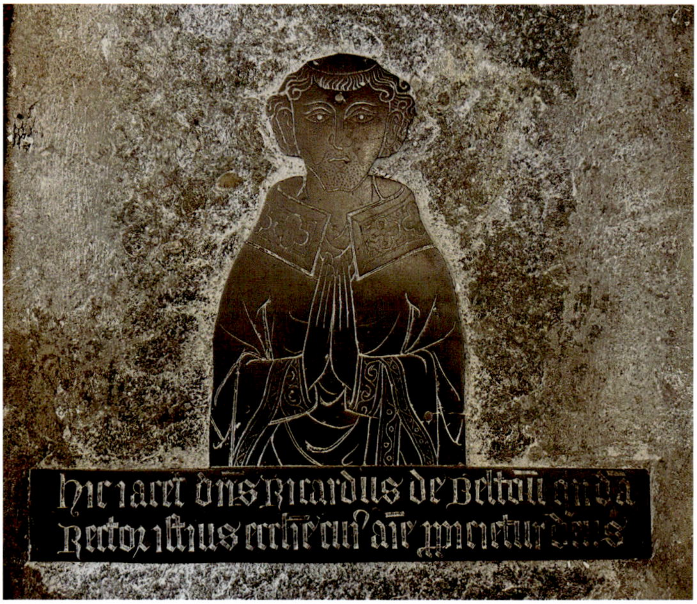

Corringham. The splendid fourteenth-century brass to Rector Richard of Belton depicts him in vestments, complete with designer stubble.

some medieval grave slabs, including one from the fourteenth century with a Lombardic inscription around the edge remembering Isabella Baud. Remarkably, the inscription is still partly infilled with lead which in most churches has been completely lost. Of about the same date is a remarkable demi-effigy in brass in the chancel which commemorates Richard of Belton, who was rector of the church at the time of the Black Death and who may have died as a result. He is depicted in his Mass vestments and the brass, which was made in London, is set into a piece of Purbeck marble. It is amongst the earliest and finest brasses in the county, and I love his fashionable designer stubble! This part of Essex is known for its riverside industries and just outside the tower is the sad grave of a fifteen-year-old messenger boy who was killed when a petrol tank exploded at the Shell Mex plant in 1924.

13. Danbury, St John the Baptist

A proud church with prominent spire, standing aloof from its village above the main road. It dates in the main from the fourteenth century, although its atmosphere is that created by extensive nineteenth-century works. The arcades are of quatrefoil cross-section which makes a change from the usual octagonal ones. It is obvious that the chancel arch is Victorian – it's of a different stone completely. In fact, there were several campaigns of work in the nineteenth century, later works often replacing some that were only a few years old. The outstanding furnishings here are three effigies of cross-legged knights dating from around 1300 and set into plain tomb recesses (see also 38. Purleigh). The crossed legs just represent the fashion of the period and aren't necessarily associated with crusaders as we used to believe. It is thought that they represent members of the St Clere family, who were benefactors to the church. They would originally have been covered

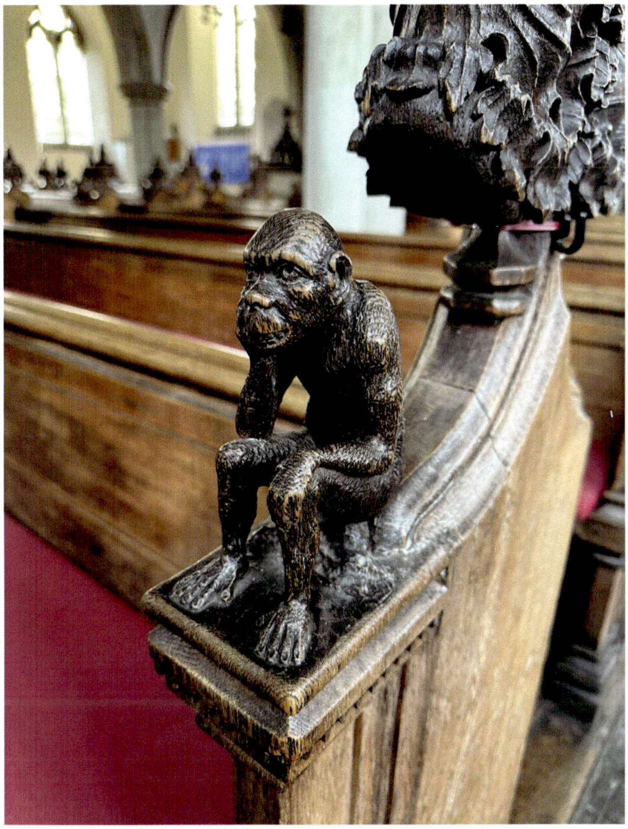

Danbury. This monkey bench end is one of a series inspired by a few surviving medieval benches at the back of the church.

in gesso (remains survive) and then painted. In the north aisle is the indent of a large cross which may well cover the actual grave of one of these knights. During the sixteenth century, the Mildmay family (Tudor courtiers) became the major landowners here and several of their monuments survive in the floor of the north aisle. Bizarrely, Humfrey Mildmay is remembered because his name was scratched on the colourful early seventeenth-century tablet to George Withers that is now under the tower. At the back of the church are a few medieval benches with elaborately carved ends and these were the inspiration for the nineteenth-century (and some later) bench ends that now fill the rest of the church. Each is a spirited design in oak with subjects ranging from a lion to a monkey, an owl to a hare. Without doubt they are the most interesting carvings in an Essex church and show how much money was spent on the church at the time. One of the reasons for this extravagance was that at that time a Bishop's Palace stood nearby, home to the bishops of Rochester from 1845 to 1892. Only the best was good enough for them, even though they had a private chapel in the palace. During that period the whole of Essex was in the diocese of Rochester, so Danbury was a useful base for conducting business north of the Thames. The church was bomb damaged in the Second World War, which explains why the mosaic-like east window in the church was installed in 1954 to the designs of Carl Edwards.

14. Debden, St Mary the Virgin

Every county has at least one church that can be described as a 'one-off' and Debden is the principal contender in Essex. As you walk down the lane the church appears below, a confection of eighteenth-century brick, battlements and pinnacles. Yet when you get nearer there is also the sense of a medieval core, and this is more apparent when you go inside for the nave and aisles are thirteenth century in date, topped and tailed by extraordinary Georgian ends. The circular piers are quite plain, except for two capitals on the south side which display leaf decoration. The windows in the aisles are medieval and there is a medieval chest, too. The later story of the church is of the collapse of a central tower, which eventually necessitated rebuilding the chancel. The Chiswell family made their money in the early eighteenth century through trade with Turkey, and in 1772 the Debden estate passed to Richard Muilman, a nephew of the Chiswells. He inherited equivalent to over £20 million in today's money and changed his name to Chiswell according to the terms of the inheritance. It was he who

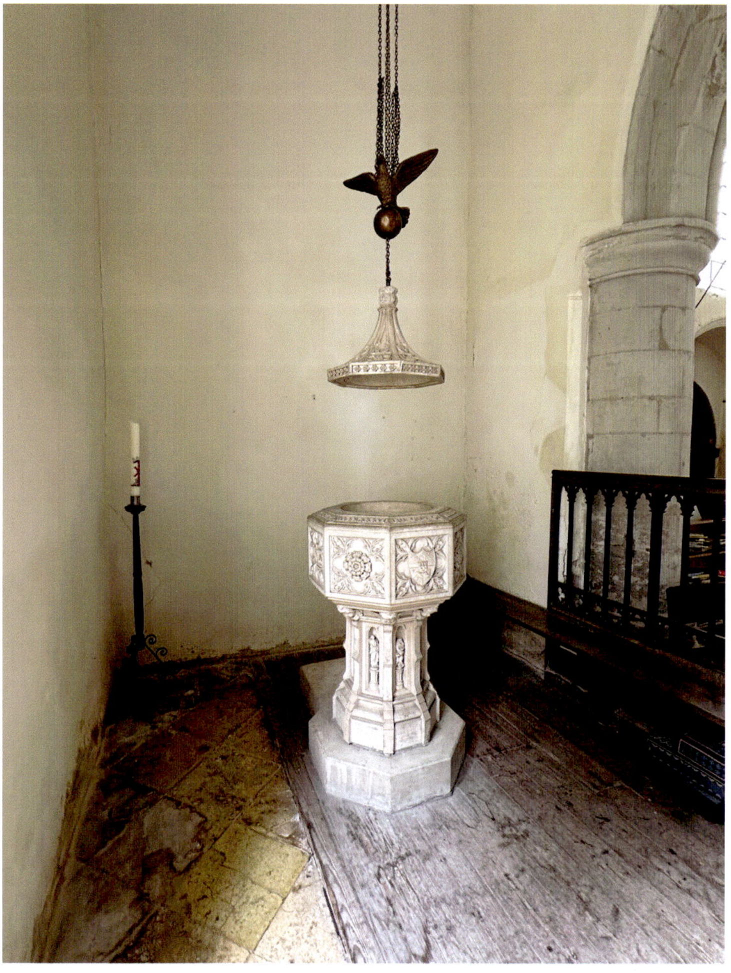

Debden. The font and cover are both constructed of artificial Coade stone. The figures around the stem depict the various virtues.

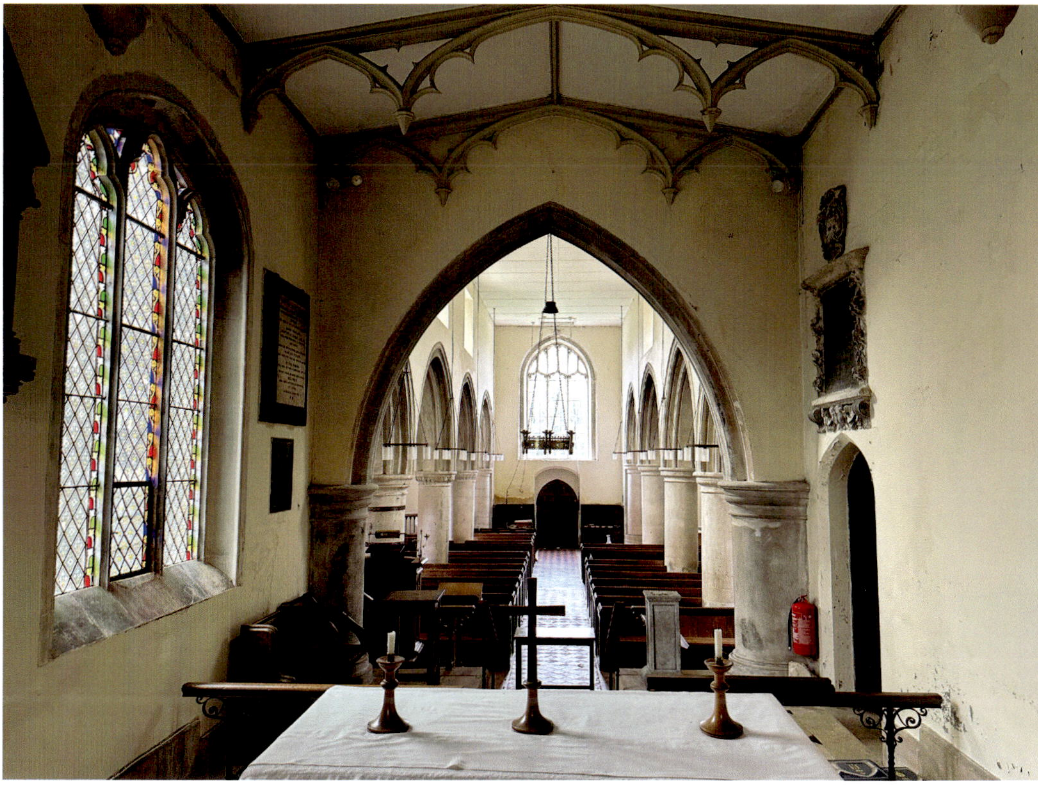

Debden. Interior looking west from the chancel showing the contrast between the Gothic chancel and the thirteenth-century piers in the nave.

built the present chancel with his large burial vault underneath, and who also commissioned the font. The chancel is octagonal in shape with a Gothic vault and deep pendants. It contains three major monuments. Firstly, to his uncle from whom he had inherited the estate: a simple oval tablet with a mourning woman and urn. Secondly, to his parents, a heraldic tablet with a draped urn. Both these are signed by the fashionable firm of King of Bath. The third monument is to Chiswell himself and is a richly canopied Gothic tomb chest probably designed by the architect of the chancel, John Carter. Sadly, Chiswell was gradually losing his fortune and shot himself. As a suicide he wouldn't have been allowed burial in the church, but as the inquest into his death recorded a verdict of 'lunacy' it was permissible. At the west end of the church is an amazing font and cover, both of which are made of Lithodipyra a form of artificial stone produced by the Coade Company of Lambeth. It is signed and dated on the base. The stem has (damaged) statues which represent the virtues, each labelled to make it easy for us to identify them. I love the tiny lion at Fortitude's feet! The south window in the south aisle is made up of Georgian glass depicting the heraldry of the Muilman, Trench and Chiswell families whose combined fortunes created this unusual interior.

15. Doddinghurst, All Saints

Set in an urban twentieth-century setting, this is a delightful church which has witnessed the vicissitudes of centuries. It dates from the thirteenth century and takes the form of a simple nave and chancel with a hefty wooden frame set into its west end to support the bell frame above, in which hang three bells. In the south wall below the belfry, is a blocked thirteenth-century-style window but the stonework is Victorian, inserted by the architect J. P. St Aubyn who replaced a lot of stonework here in his heavy-handed restoration of 1887. Genuinely thirteenth century is the south doorway, with colonettes and some dogtooth moulding just peeping out behind. It has been preserved by the huge Tudor porch which gives the church such character. Just inside the doorway is a chunky fourteenth-century font which must have looked splendid when new, with all its carvings painted in bright colour. Inside, the massive frame for the belfry can't be missed. Unusually the arch-braces at the base come to the church door to counteract any lean into the building. The roof structure of the nave is completely medieval with prominent crown posts, but as soon as we reach the chancel everything has been renewed. In fact, the contrast between the medieval rood beam and the timber framing behind couldn't be starker.

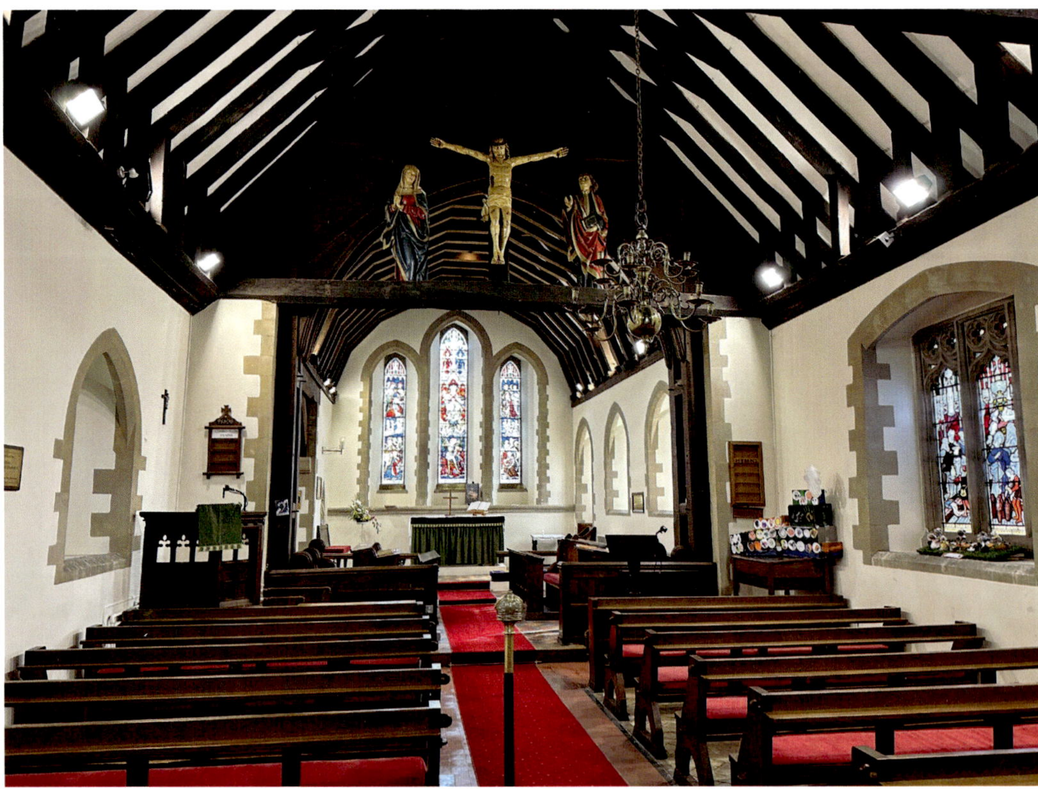

Doddinghurst. Interior looking east showing the medieval rood figures imported from the Continent. The nave roof is medieval and the chancel roof is of 1887.

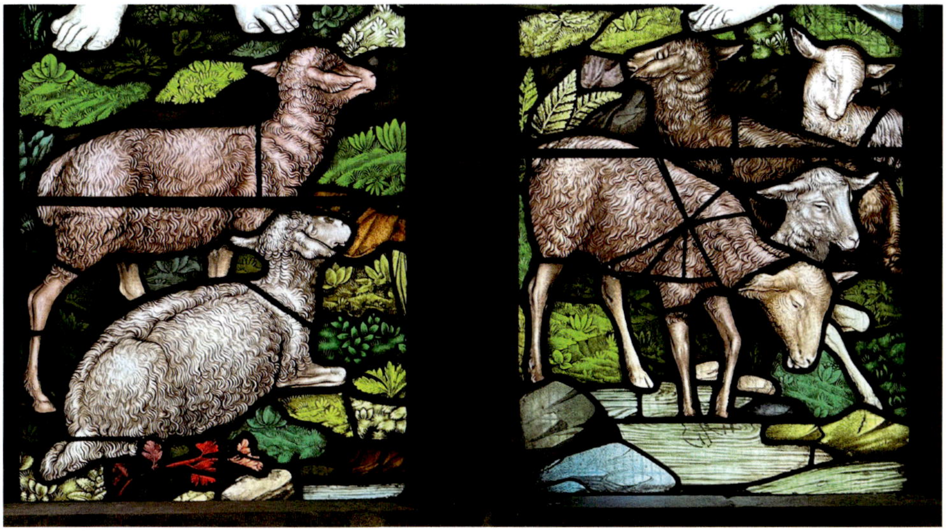

Doddinghurst. Detail of a window by A. O. Hemming, 'Feed My Sheep'.

The rood figures themselves were a nineteenth-century gift. They are of German manufacture of the early sixteenth century and make a fine contrast to most Essex roods where the figures are Victorian. Unusually, all the stained glass is designed by the same artist and installed at the same time. As part of a church restoration donations towards windows in memory of a late relative were often invited but here the rector and his family paid for most of them. The designer was Alfred Octavious Hemming, who had a studio on London's Marylebone Road. Each depicts a scene from the Life of Christ (which together with the gift of the rood suggests a high Church influence at the time of the restoration). My two favourites are the sheep at the base of the west window (Christ says to Peter 'Feed my Sheep') and the Marriage at Cana in a south window where Christ turns water into wine. It is always a tricky subject to portray and here Hemming has it just right.

16. East Mersea, St Edmund King and Martyr

I find that islands are full of surprises and Mersea gives us one of the most atmospheric churches in Essex. The tower on its diminutive chequerboard plinth is of stone rubble and wouldn't look out of place in Kent with its north-east stair turret. Here it is given an exotic twist by a palm tree growing against its south face. The two huge wooden-framed windows of the nave date from the eighteenth century when 'churchwarden repairs' were carried out to ensure that the ratepayers of the parish had their contribution kept to a minimum. The jaunty classically inspired porch hides a medieval door that now opens in two leaves. The church is a light open space, unlike the crowded interior depicted in an old photograph taken before the box pews were removed. The dominant feature is the seventeenth-century pulpit with a sounding board and the iron stand for the parson's hourglass. The brick floor gives a rustic feel

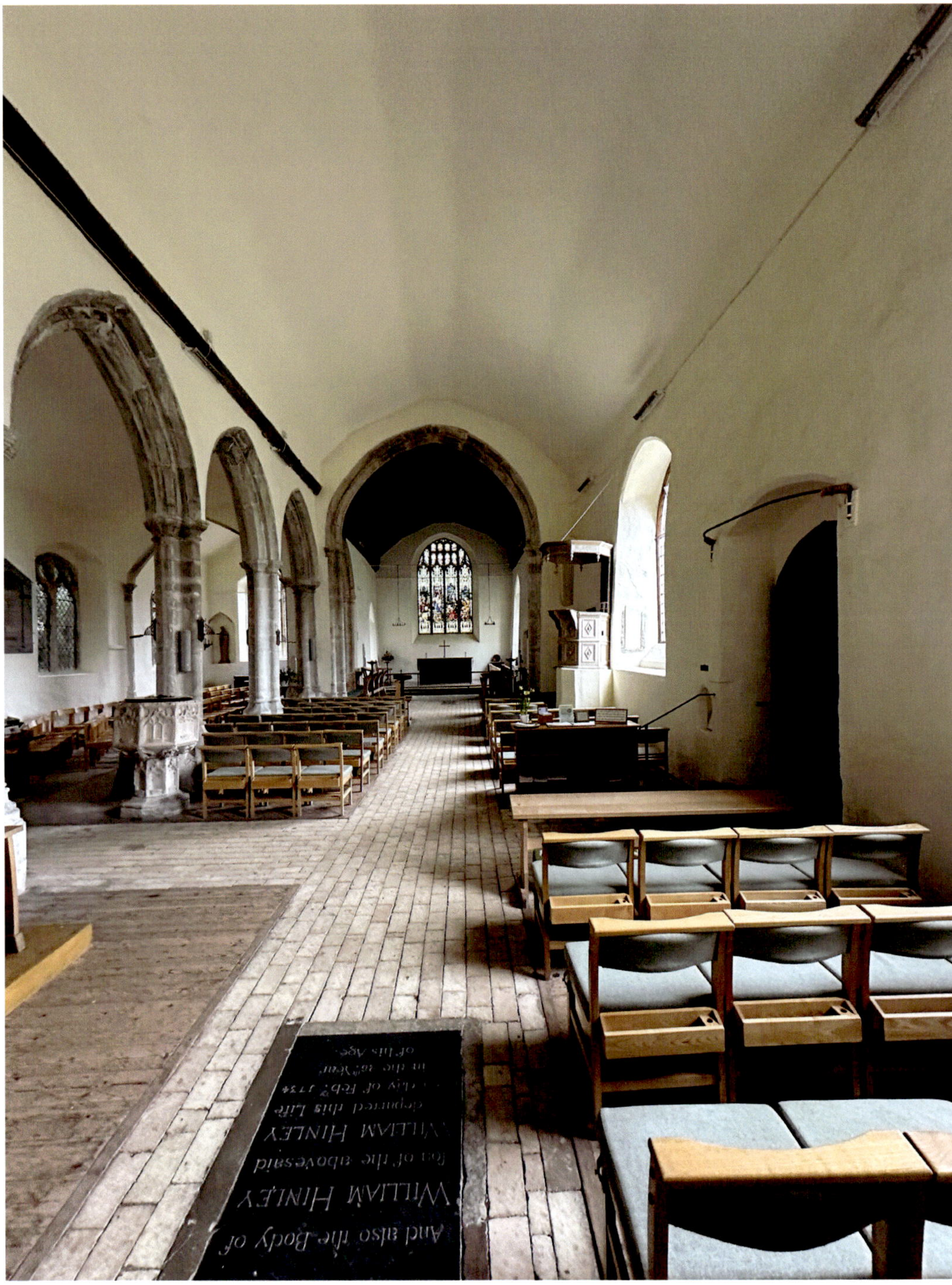

East Mersea. Interior looking east with brick floor. The north arcade was built in the fifteenth century on a grand scale leading into a generous north aisle.

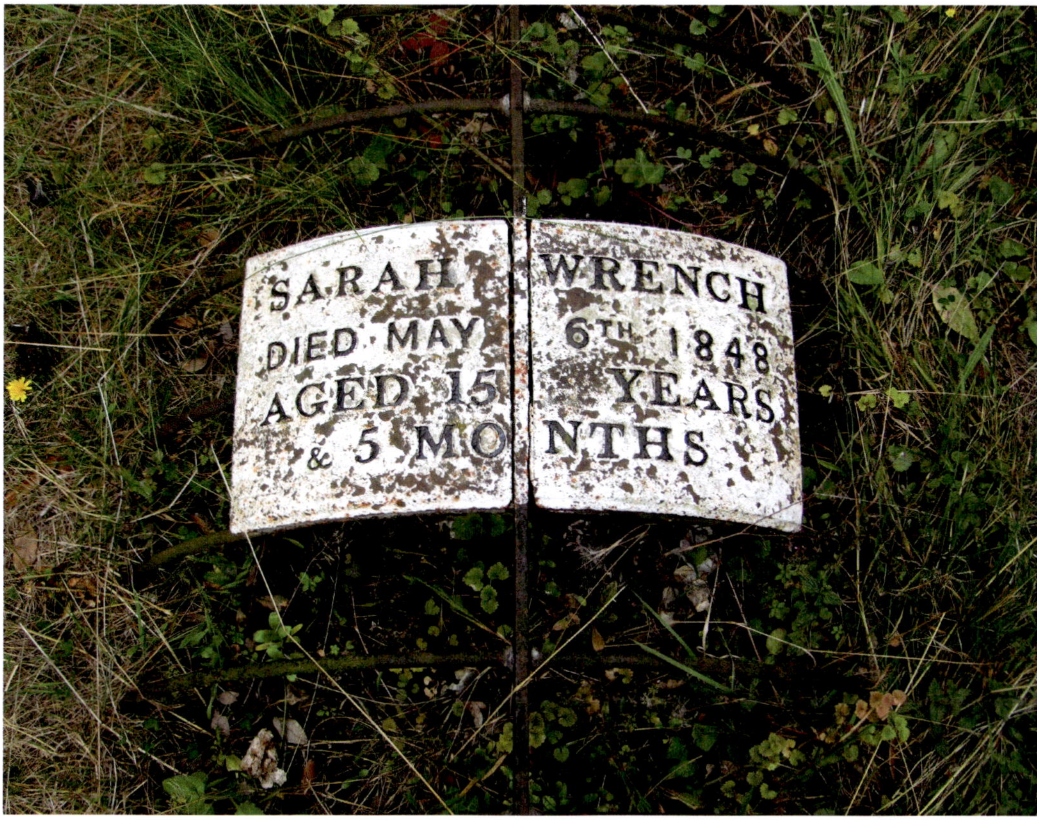

East Mersea. To the north of the church is a metal mortsafe to deter grave robbers covering the grave of Sarah Wrench. (Image by Simon Knott)

and, in the chancel, contains a brass with long inscription to Mawdlyn Owtred (d. 1572) wife of the rector. Only the patron, rector and their families were permitted burial in such an important part of the church. The rhyme includes the line that she was buried 'in December month when days are colde' and one can imagine they are in this exposed place. The church was extended by the addition of a north aisle in the fifteenth century and the colossal arcades seem completely out of scale. Its donor must have been very proud of his work. A tiny hagioscope joins the site of its eastern altar with the altar in the chancel. In an area without good quality building stone, we expect to find wooden memorials and a particularly fine heraldic example is on the south wall. It is a heraldic shield to Edward Bellamie, fishmonger, who died in 1656. Its frame carries a skull and crossbones design, and as he is described as a lieutenant-colonel we know that he fought in the Wars of the Three Kingdoms. The church contains a fine collection of Continental glass panels, my favourite being an archer in the north aisle. In the churchyard on the north side of the church is a rare surviving mortsafe over the grave of Sarah Wrench, who died at the age of fifteen in 1848, the iron cage designed to deter graverobbers.

17. Fairstead, St Mary

The Essex Way long-distance footpath runs through the churchyard of St Mary's and many a hiker will have taken shelter and rest within its walls. This is a Norman church where the builders used a lot of Roman brick in their construction. In a flint area like this, making a corner was always a challenge and rather than import stone from elsewhere it was easier to use what they found at hand. Wherever you look, inside and out, Roman brick has been used; only the outer quoins of the chancel, rebuilt in the thirteenth century when money was more plentiful, use stone. Inside, the star attraction are the wall paintings high above the chancel arch. In this location the Doom is the most commonly found subject, but here we are looking at a painting from the early fourteenth century before the Doom became omnipresent, and it represents scenes from the Passion. All the major parts of the story can be discerned, but I am always intrigued by the scene where the Crown of Thorns is placed on Christ's head. It may be just the way in which the image has faded, but the figure looks to me as if 'she' has stepped out of a Lowrey painting. The nave contains other paintings too. There are the remains of two sets of Consecration crosses, and it is easy to see the difference between the two styles of cross used. There are also remains of some post-Reformation

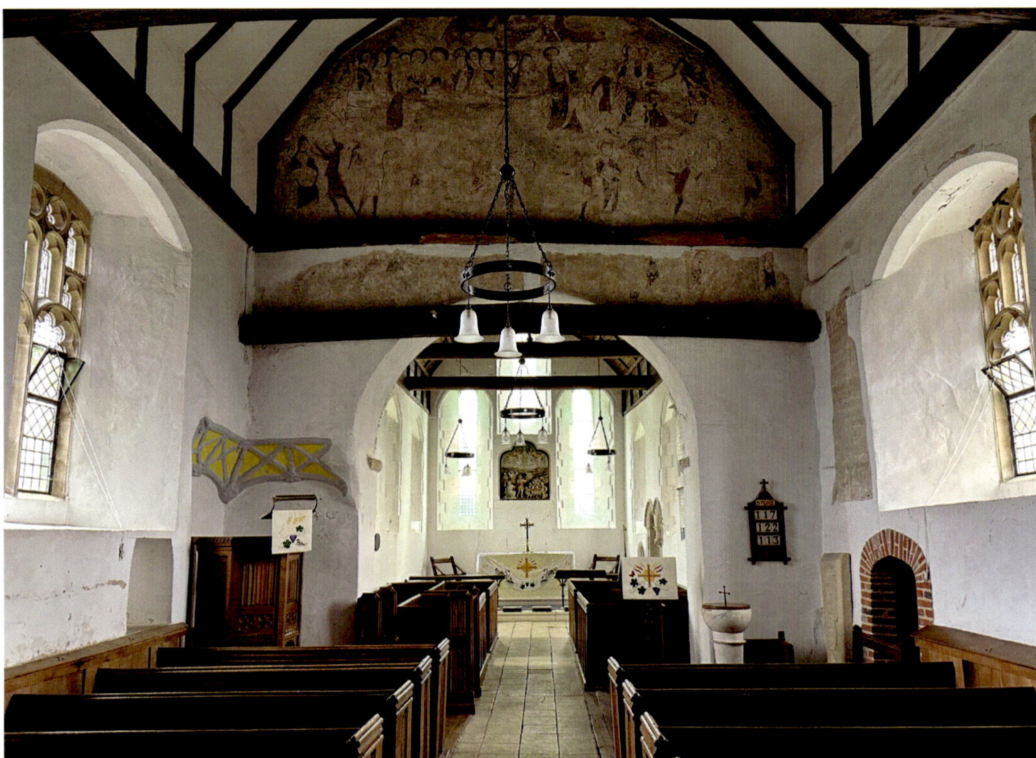

Fairstead. Interior looking east showing the wall paintings over the chancel arch depicting scenes from the Passion of Christ. The medieval vault now painted yellow over the pulpit gave honour to an altar that once stood here.

black letter inscriptions, including one which covers the former opening to the rood loft. A careful inspection will reveal a vertical crack where the edge of the upper doorway runs. On the north side of the church is an unusual carved and vaulted recess for a nave altar that stood where the pulpit now is, its vaulting painted brilliant yellow. On the opposite side of the church is a thirteenth-century stone coffin lid now affixed to the wall. Much of its carving has been destroyed but a double omega symbol survives and tells us that this was probably made in Barnack, near Peterborough, and brought here by a raft up the rivers Chelmer and Ter. The chancel contains a simple two-seat sedilia from the thirteenth century whilst at the back of the church is a huge dug-out chest of similar date.

18. Fingringhoe, St Andrew

A quintessentially English village with church, school and pub in close proximity on high ground above the Roman River near its junction with the River Colne. The most obvious feature of the exterior is the fourteenth-century tower which is formed of bands of flint (see 12. Corringham) standing on a plinth of chequerboard flints. It makes quite a statement as you enter the village. The porch displays St Michael and the dragon in the spandrels of its doorway and hides a south door with its large late medieval closing ring which predates the use of latches. As you step down into the church you see extensive remains of medieval wall paintings, although sadly most are very faded. However, the best medieval feature is the statue of St Margaret on the splay of the north window. Although half her head is missing this is a rare survival, having been carved in the fifteenth century and walled up at the Reformation only to be discovered in 1968. Amazingly, the statue retains traces of its original colour. Another medieval statue was discovered about the same time, a statue of God the Father which is now set into the wall above the pulpit. It may once have depicted the Holy Trinity but if it once did the requisite dove has since disappeared. The church contains remarkably few monuments but over the north chancel door is an alabaster monument to George Frere (d. 1655) of Fingringhoe Hall, his hand resting on a skull to remind us of mortality. The inscription tells us he was a London merchant and a shield at the base shows a sailing ship with a seahorse, the emblem of the Levant Company. Unusually, on either side of the main text is a later inscription recording that the monument was repaired in 1779 by the churchwardens Thomas Cooper and Benjamin Page. Mounted on the arch between chancel and south chapel is a very late memorial brass depicting John Allen and his daughter. The inscription plate is boldly inscribed but carries no date. It is a palimpsest and you can flip it on the modern hinge to find a Latin inscription on the reverse. This slightly older inscription (about 1600) is inscribed with the monogram 'WR' and was a piece of work that went wrong so the metal plate was reused on the other side for Mr Allen. Two other objects caught my eye. The cushion on the sedilia is embroidered with the names of the four dioceses that have covered the county of Essex – London, Rochester, St Albans and Chelmsford. At the back of the church is a colourful royal arms with an inscription recording its donation to the church 1763. However, the arms are those of the early part of the reign of Queen Anne (see 40. Rayleigh) so they must have originally hung elsewhere.

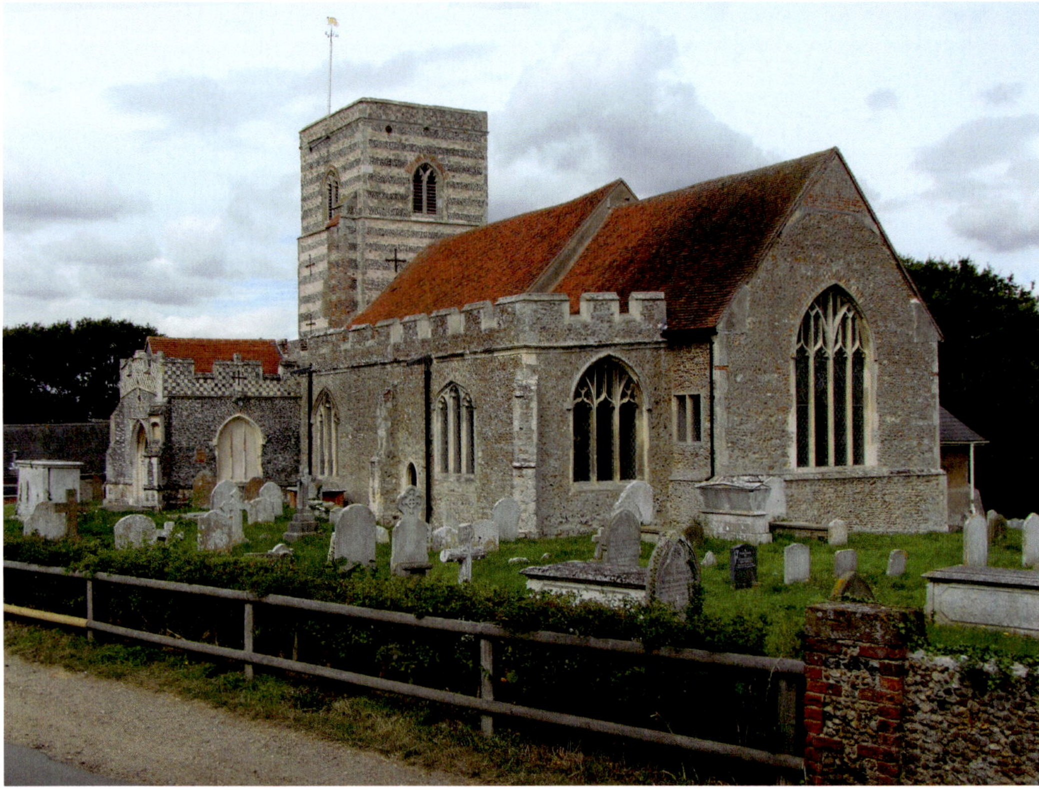

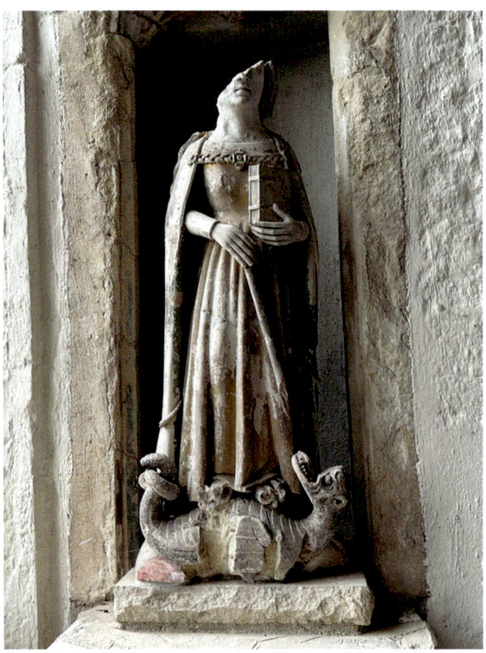

Above: Fingringhoe. Exterior from the south-east showing the flint and ragstone banding on the tower which is common in churches either side of the Thames. The porch is more typically East Anglian with chequer decoration.

Left: Fingringhoe. This medieval statue of St Margaret and the dragon was discovered walled up, having probably been hidden there during the Reformation. The paint is original.

19. Gestingthorpe, St Mary

An intriguing church in both its architecture and furnishings, St Mary's sits on a prominent bluff with wide-ranging views to the south and east. The tower is of superb quality, built of brick about 1500, with decorative diapering in black brick on the walls. It has deep corner buttresses and a prominent stair turret on the south-east corner. Above the bell openings is a frieze of trefoil headed arches and at each corner there is a prominent crocketed spirelet. The sixteenth-century double hammerbeam roof of the nave is spectacular and apparently carries the names of those who paid for it, but I've not yet found them! I suggest you take binoculars. In the chancel is a very fine memorial to John Sparrow, who died in 1626, which takes a familiar form of the deceased kneeling, but instead of kneeling at a prayer desk he is in front of his helmet. Indeed, the whole memorial shows images of war – armour, standards and drums, and is worthy of close inspection. There is still some residual original colour. At the rear of the church and set either side of the towering red-brick tower arch are Georgian paintings of Moses and Aaron which most churches displayed in the eighteenth century, but of which few examples survive in such good condition. The object most people come to Gestingthorpe to see is the brass inscription on the north wall to Captain Lawrence Edward Oates who famously left his companions on the

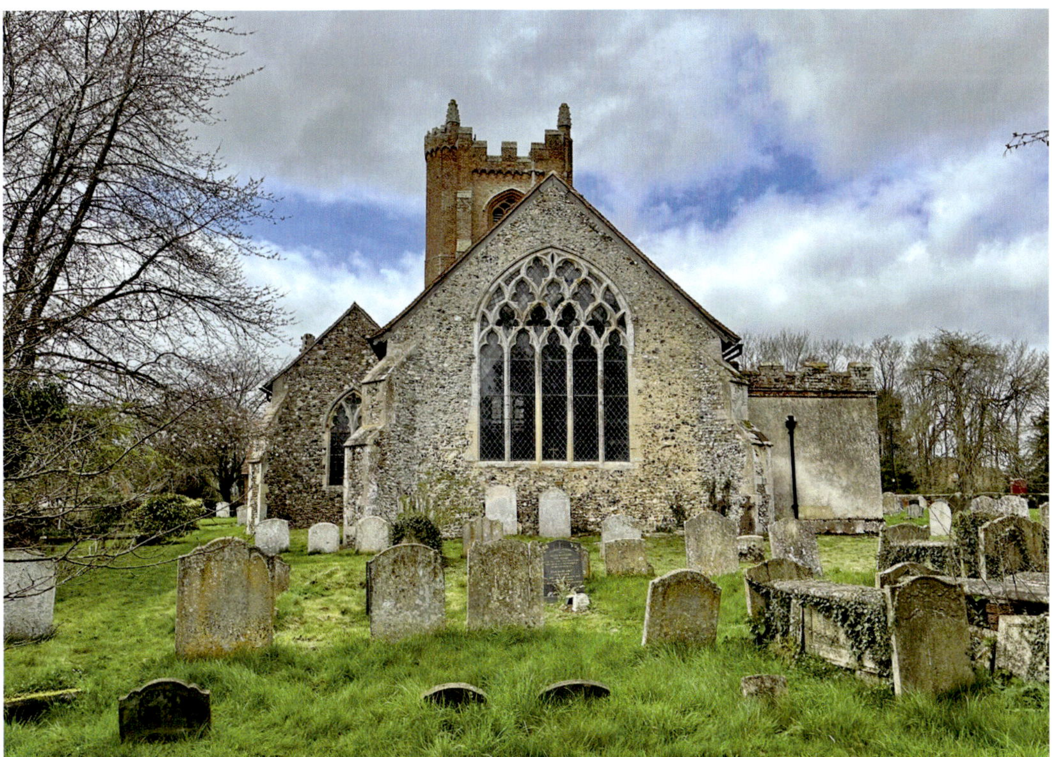

Gestingthorpe. The large east window dates from about 1290 and can be described as 'reticulated' in design. The Tudor tower peeps out behind.

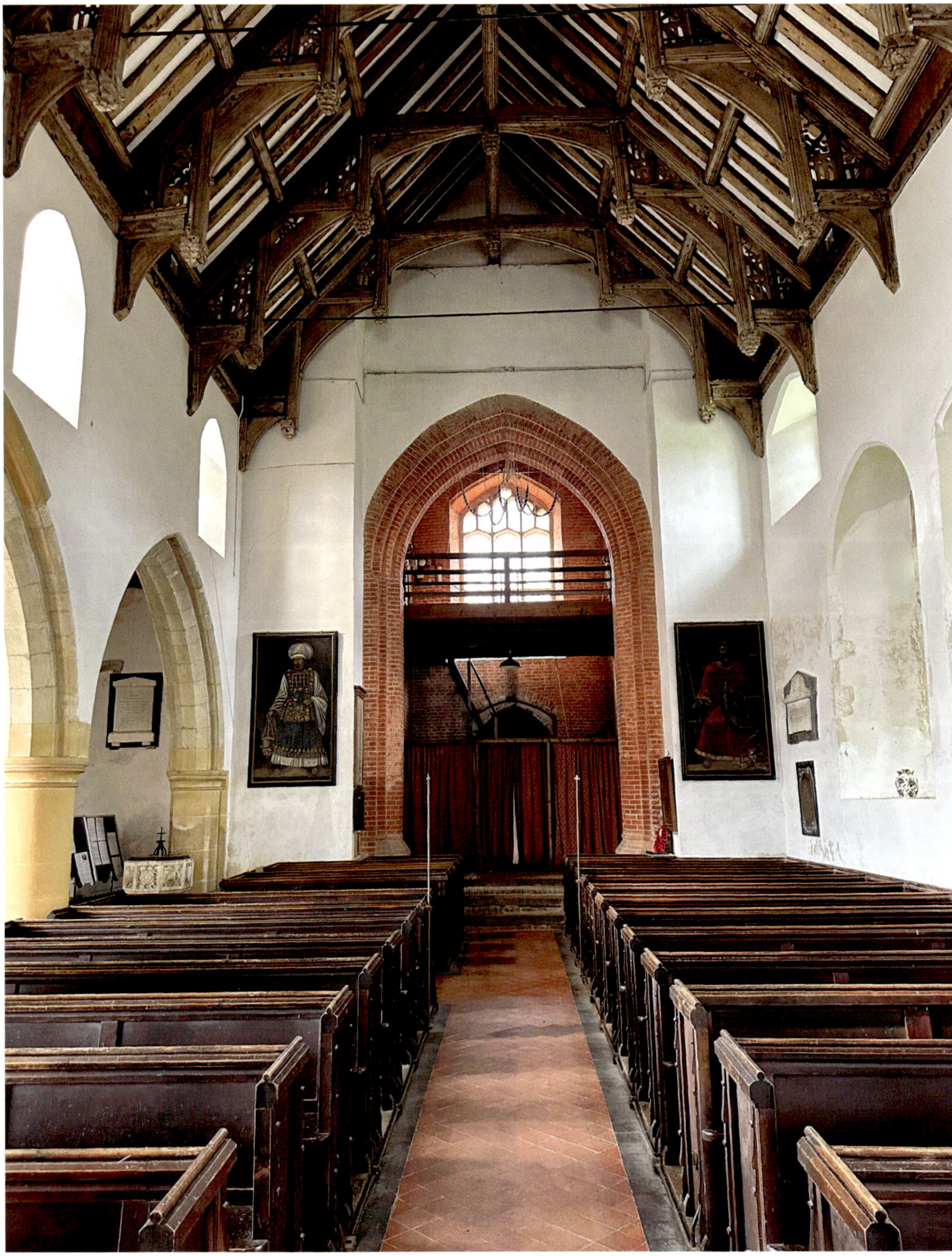

Gestingthorpe. When the tower was added to the church in the early sixteenth century, this tall arch was constructed to join it to the nave. Either side are pictures of Moses and Aaron dating from the eighteenth century.

1912 Antarctic Expedition to give them a better chance of survival with the lines 'I am just going outside; I may be some time'. The pulpit is of the rare tapering form that became popular in the late nineteenth century when the Arts and Crafts movement was in its infancy. The stonework of the east window dates from the late thirteenth century and is what is known as a 'reticulated' design. The tracery at the top reminds one of a fishing net but the design does not fill the window, leaving small oddly shaped areas. Later windows of this style take the net design right to the edges of the window, showing that this was an experimental period. It is best seen from the churchyard.

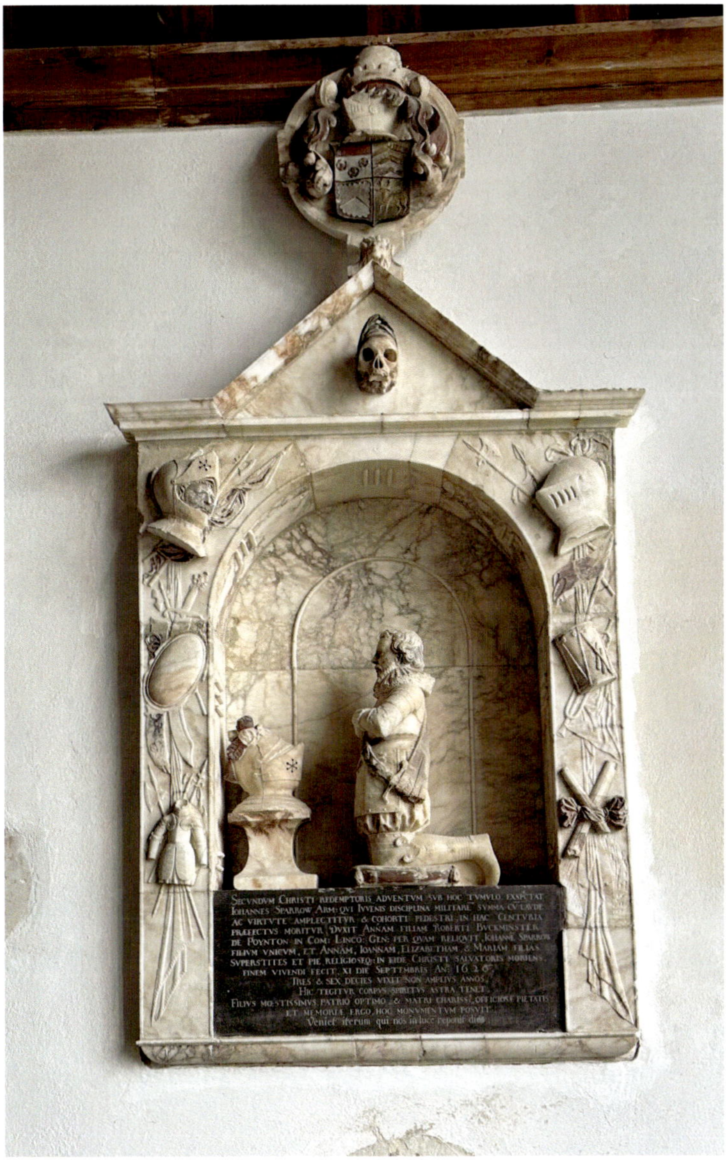

Gestingthorpe. The Sparrow monument is interesting as he kneels in front of his helm surrounded by military references, rather than in front of a prayer desk.

20. Gosfield, St Catherine

The church stands on the edge of the park of Gosfield Hall, the owners of which created the building we see today. A walk around the outside will set the scene showing a flint tower and nave of the fifteenth century and a chancel and north chapel of Tudor brick. You step into a cavernous space, emphasised by the tall tower arch which frames the font, and by a wooden brace which runs near the west end of the nave with charming pierced spandrels. There is a collection of post-Reformation godly texts painted on the wall and two ranks of box pews. On the north wall, above the pulpit, is an unusual private pew set into a glazed arch with three opening shutters at the base to allow the occupants to have a view into the church. It would have been entered via the north chapel and a staircase to enable its owners to come and go without having to mingle with their tenants. It houses one of the finest monuments in Essex, which remembers John Knight (d. 1733) by the Flemish sculptor John Michael Rysbrack, but you will need to make arrangements to see it as it is kept locked, though you can get a peek through the glazed screen. The chancel and north chapel contain three chest tombs. To the south of the altar is the tomb of Thomas Rolf (d. 1440) with a brass which shows him in his robes of a lawyer. Whilst the effigy itself is not high quality, the same cannot be said for the Latin inscription plate, which is a calligrapher's dream of swirls and pauses. The two other tomb chests are 100 years later and only have the fragmentary remains of brasses set within them. The east wall of the north chapel is panelled with some remarkable mid-sixteenth-century Renaissance carvings. Each panel is different and subjects range from foliage spewers to some highly sexualised dancing figures – even the angels are shown as male and female! It must surely have come from Gosfield Hall. In the churchyard is the grave of big band leader Jack Hylton (1892–1965).

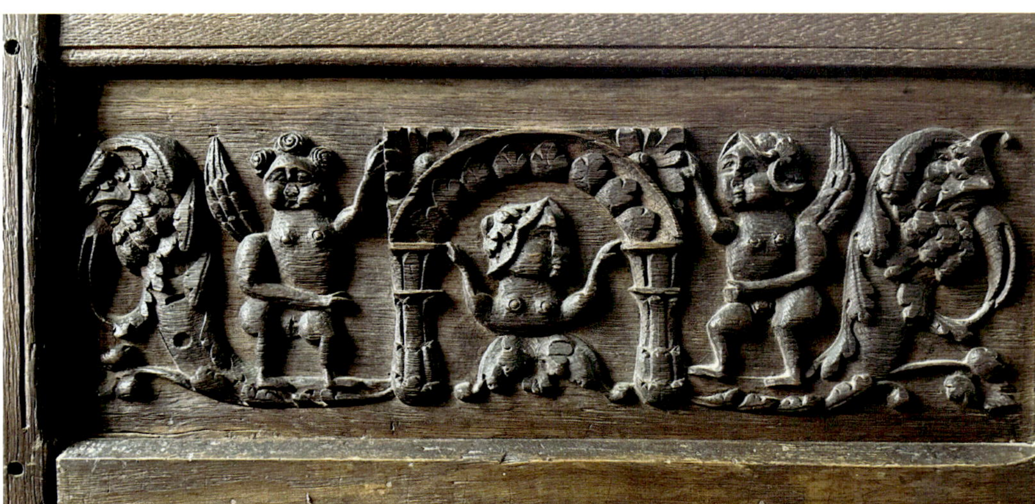

Gosfield. This Continental panelling in the north chapel which includes sexually explicit carvings must once have graced a domestic building.

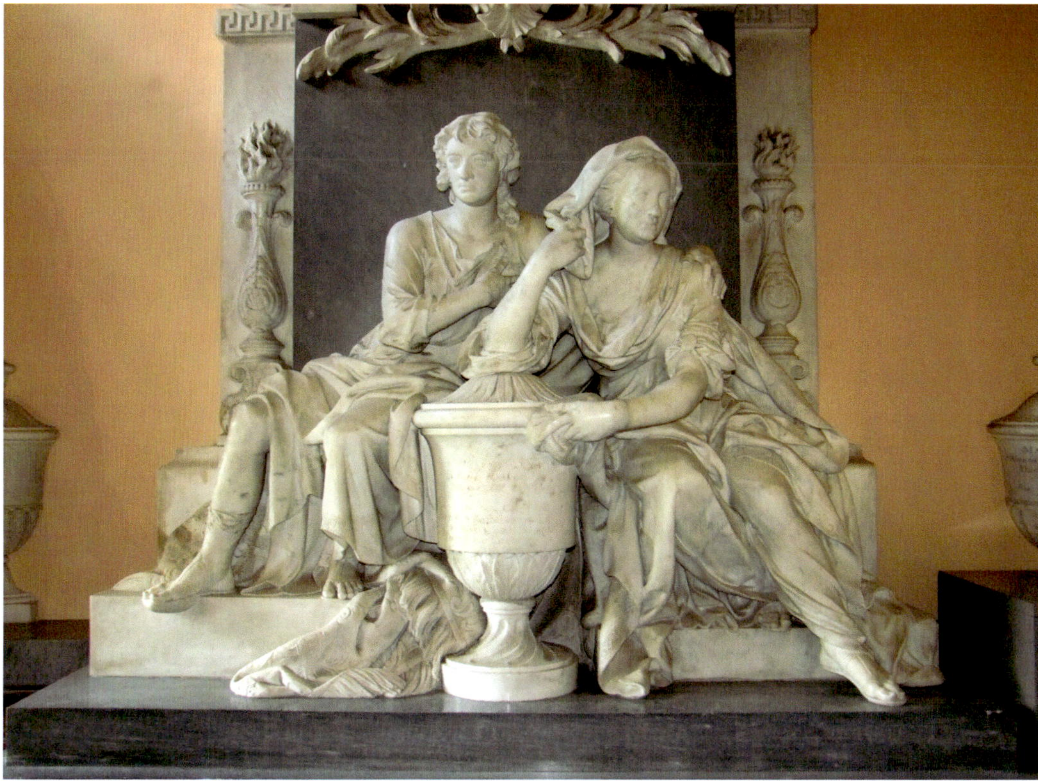

Gosfield. The monument to John Knight (d. 1733) by Rysbrack stands in its own private pew to the north of the church. (Image by Simon Knott)

21. Great Bromley, St George

Most medieval churches in Essex are built of stone rubble, laid in horizontal courses and originally covered with lime mortar to make the wall weathertight. Where churches were later extended, at a time when more money was available, these extensions were often in expensive flint flushwork whose intricate patterns were never meant to be covered up. Here at Great Bromley, we can see both techniques, although much of the early work is no longer covered with mortar. Indeed, it is the flint south porch and clerestory which make the church memorable. The latter throws light inside onto a spectacular double hammerbeam roof installed in the late fifteenth century, and some of its original painted decoration can be seen in the two eastern bays. The south arcade dates from the fourteenth century and the capital nearest the door contains some distinctive carvings, from a stately lion to a woman being swallowed by a dragon and another whose face is being eaten by a dragon and a toad! It was carved to stop evil spirits entering the church via the south door. Like all stonework in the church, it would have been brightly painted. Further east, at waist height, you can just pick out a person's leg on another pier, whilst a tiny fragment of painting survives high on the south aisle wall. In front of the Holy

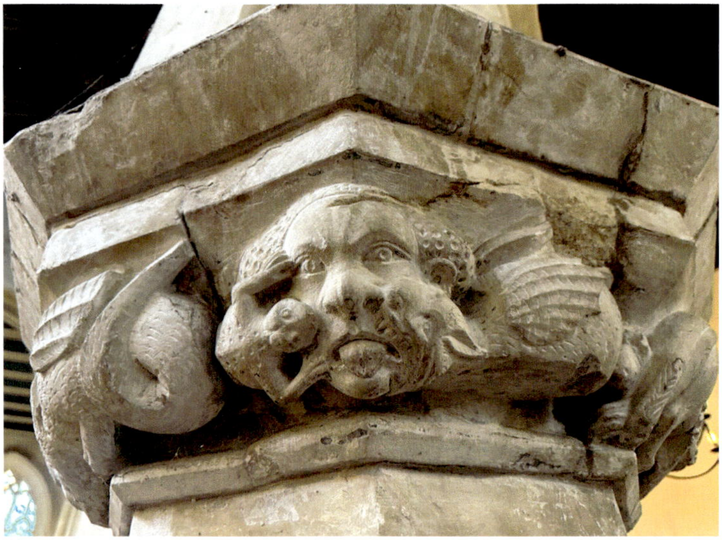

Great Bromley. This capital depicts a face being eaten by a dragon and a toad and was intended to keep evil spirits from entering the church by the south door.

Table in the south chapel is one of the most important memorial brasses in Essex. It commemorates William Byschopton, rector of the church who died in 1432, depicted in his vestments with a ribbon inscription issuing from his mouth. Sadly, over half the inscription at the base has been lost, as have the finials at the top of the composition, but even so it represents the finest example of medieval art. Above the Holy Table is a reredos of Ancaster stone by Suffolk sculptor Antonia Hockton, installed in 2015, which represents the River of Life. The memorial tablets in the chapel represent the Hanson family, the inscriptions showing that they were much travelled in business and military service. The best is to William Hanson, who was killed aged just twenty-five during the Peninsula Wars, which shows one of his fellow soldiers kneeling beneath the Union Flag. It is signed by John Bacon the Younger, whose studio in London was not far from the Hanson's London house in Russell Square. The east window of 1953, replacing one blown out in the war, depicts Christ in Glory and was designed by Gerald Smith of the A. K. Nicholson Studios.

22. Great Burstead, St Mary Magdalene

This large medieval church stands in a conservation area and large graveyard, on a site that is reputed to have had a church since the earliest days of Christianity in Essex. The earliest feature of the present building is the small round-headed window in the north wall of the nave and the yew tree to the south of the church might be as old! It is much shored up and some of its earlier supports, in the form of iron chains, have now grown into the branches. The church stands on a north–south slope so the ground to the north is very much higher than that on the south, which no doubt caused problems as the church expanded in size during the fourteenth and fifteenth centuries. The prominent west tower is built of Kentish ragstone and proudly displays its putlog holes where the original wooden scaffolding beams were built into the walls as they went up. When the beams were removed the holes were left in case the tower needed scaffolding for repairs later. You step down into

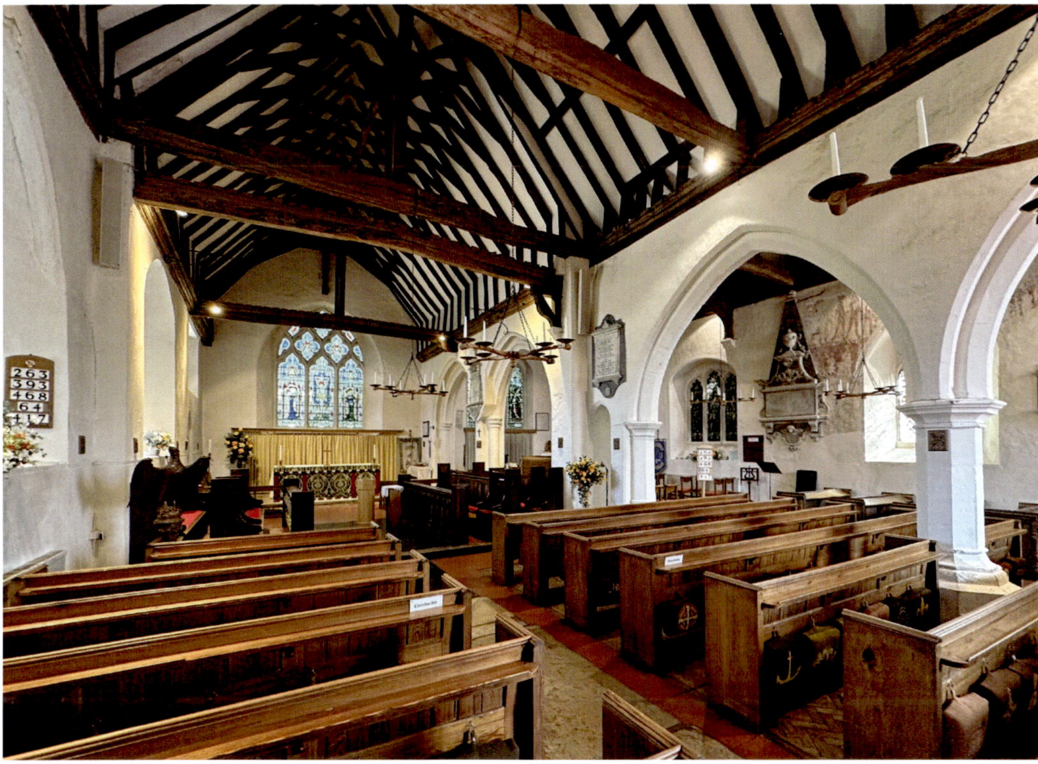

Above: Great Burstead. Interior showing the Norman nave, fourteenth-century south aisle and fifteenth-century chapel. The crownpost roof has crenellated tie beams in the chancel.

Right: Great Burstead. This spectacular window commemorates a local man who was one of the earliest settlers in the New World, Christopher Martin.

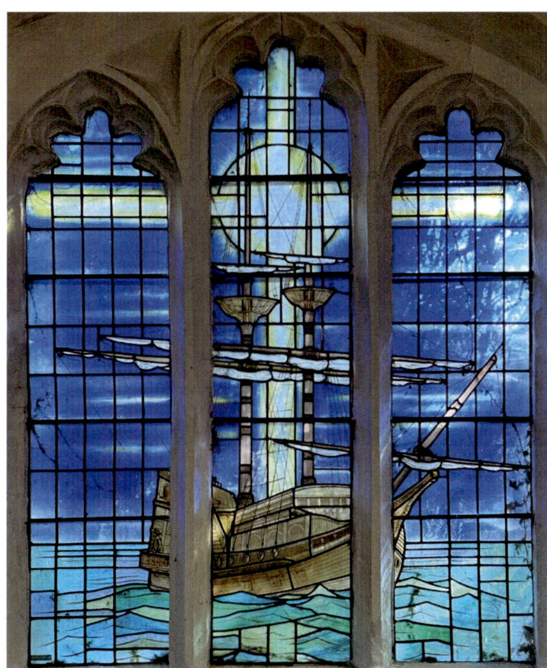

the church from a large fourteenth-century porch and by looking at the base of the nave arcade you can see just how high the floor level was in the original church for the bases of the piers are incredibly tall. The south chapel is of a much higher architectural quality than the chancel. Above its east window inside is a carved representation of the royal arms of England, whilst outside it has a course of knapped flints along its south wall and a chequerboard of flint and stone on its east wall, representing a very expensive project. Inside the chapel its main feature is the *Mayflower* memorial window, designed by Matthew Lloyd-Winder and erected in 2003 to commemorate Christopher Martin, a churchwarden of Great Burstead, who sailed to the New World on the *Mayflower* as one of its officials. Sadly, he died within two months of his arrival. Below it is a famous dug-out chest which some people think may be as early as the twelfth century. There are several monuments of note – Sarah Cooke died of 'that mercyless distemper the Small Pox' whilst Samuel Bridge was a 'painfull, powerful preacher'. The royal arms, which now bear the initials of Queen Victoria, but which are known to have been painted for George III in 1795, are unusual in not having the Lion and Unicorn standing facing each other, but instead almost seem in play. The south wall has a large display of fourteenth-century wall paintings, many in tiny scenes that are difficult to identify.

23. Great Sampford, St Michael

Majestically standing on a rise (as so many medieval churches dedicated to St Michael do) this noble building is all about the architecture and dates from the glory days of church building, just before the Black Death. Money was plentiful via individual donors and stonemasons were delighting in what we now call the 'Decorated' style of architecture, the second of our Gothic forms. In areas where good quality stone was plentiful, it gives us superb carving; here in Essex, where that stone had to be brought from elsewhere at vast expense, is as good as it gets. At first, we should look at the south chapel. Its east window is of the period before we invented hood moulds to protect the glass, and is formed of two lights with a quatrefoil above and, as a single insertion, a sexfoil opening above. To the modern eye it looks unfinished as we are so used to seeing windows with hood moulds, but it is an important stage in the development of window tracery. The huge window in the south wall of the chapel is now blocked in with brick but must once have been spectacular – far more window than wall. We enter the church through the south porch where the original medieval door survives, its surface pitted with literally hundreds of nails showing us where legal notices have been displayed for over 600 years. The arcades between the aisles are of different designs, but probably only two generations apart. The north aisle has quatrefoil section piers whilst the south aisle has the standard later fourteenth-century octagons. It is here, where the south aisle joins the chapel, that we find the two elaborately carved capitals. That on the south side is the more interesting as it shows a man being spoken to by an owl representing 'wisdom' and a demon representing 'folly'. I wonder which one he will adopt? This quality of carving is rare in Essex. Then we enter the chancel which is lined with blank wall arcading. Although it provides a set of three sedilia in the sanctuary, the other arches are purely decorative, to enhance the status of the chancel. Interestingly, when the Victorians changed the

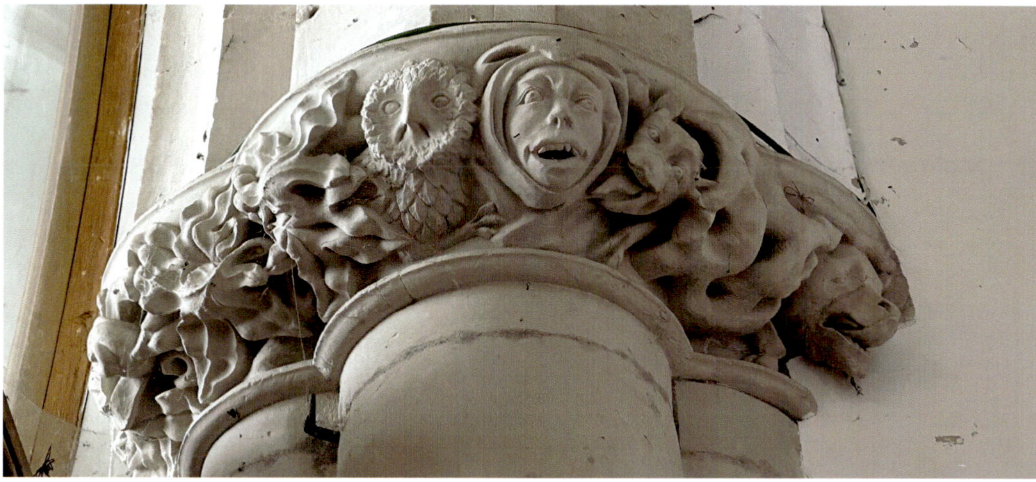

Above: Great Sampford. This fourteenth-century capital shows a man having to decide between the wisdom of an owl or the folly of a monster.

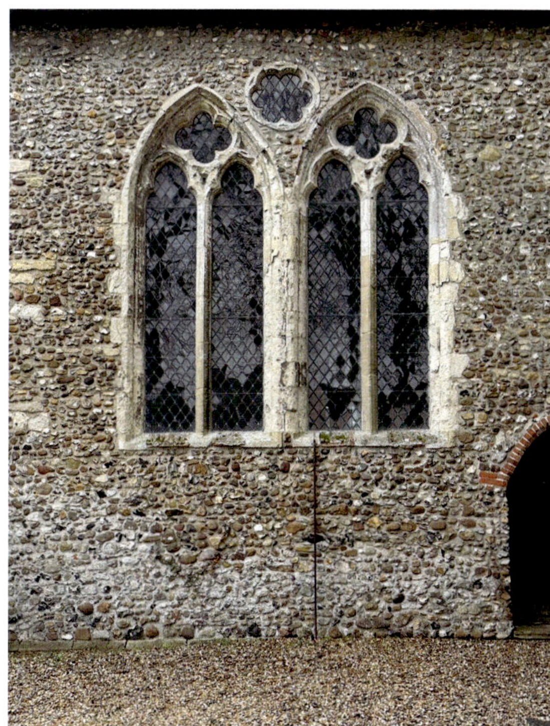

Right: Great Sampford. This window dates from the thirteenth century and is unusual in having no hood mould over the openings to protect the glass from water running over it.

floor level in the chancel they kept the floor in front of the sedilia at a useable height, when in so many churches they changed the floor levels with no regard to keeping sedilia in use. In the north west corner of the chancel you can see where a low side window was incorporated into the blank arcading. Before you leave look for the Georgian Schoolmaster's Desk reminding us that early schools often met in church and the lovely hutch cupboard against the west wall.

24. Great Waltham, St Mary and St Lawrence

In common with many Essex churches, it is the reuse of Roman brick which is remembered here. In the exterior east wall it is still possible to see the blocked round headed windows of brick which date from the Norman period, made redundant when the large fourteenth-century window was inserted in the wall. This is a huge church, the result of the addition of a south aisle in the fourteenth century and a north aisle in 1875. It is the glorious collection of memorials that the visitor comes to see. The large alabaster monument to Sir Anthony Everard (d. 1614) now stands in the north aisle but originally stood against the nave wall. Unusually it incorporates two windows which contain heraldic glass. Sir Anthony is nonchalantly looking away whilst his wife, on a lower shelf, stares out at the viewer. There are three inscription tablets, one set into a glorious sunburst. Touchingly, the base of the monument shows three dead babies, only one of which, Richard, lived long enough to be named. The other two are referred to only by the sad word 'Anonymous'. Ninety years later Hugh Everard was killed aged just sixteen in the Great Storm of 1703 when the ship on which he was sailing sank on the Goodwin Sands leaving thousands of sailors dead. His memorial in the south aisle tells the story of his promising early life and has, at the base, a depiction of his ship foundering on the sands. Nearby is another memorial with a sorry tale. Peter Curgenven was a merchant engaged in the East India Trade. In 1720, having made his fortune he decided to return to England but on the way his ship, the *Charlotte*, was captured by Kanhoji Angre of the Maratha Navy and he was thrown in prison. After nine years he was released and started out for England. Sadly, just before he arrived in London a vein in his leg burst and surgeons recommended he have his leg amputated, after which he only survived twelve days. Another memorial in the south aisle, of coloured marble, commemorates several members of the Sorell family, and the ledgerstone which covers their vault can be found in the floor nearby. A third prominent family, the Tufnells, are recalled by the six wonderful hatchments carried in their funeral processions that now hang in the nave. Look out for their crest which is an arm holding a cutlass!

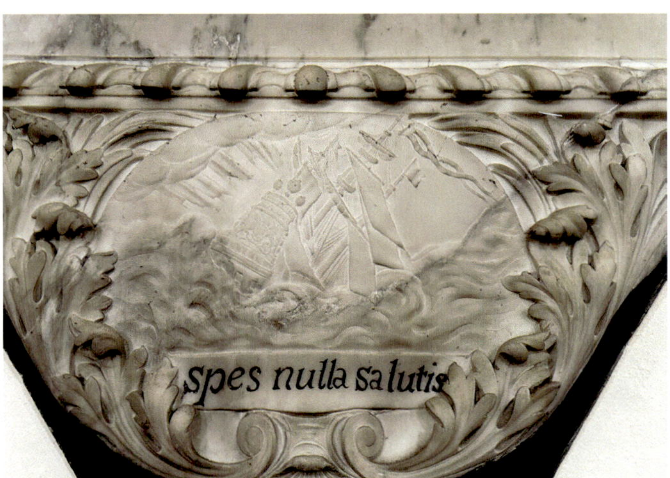

Great Waltham. The church contains many fine memorials including this to Hugh Everard whose ship ran aground on the Goodwin Sands in 1703.

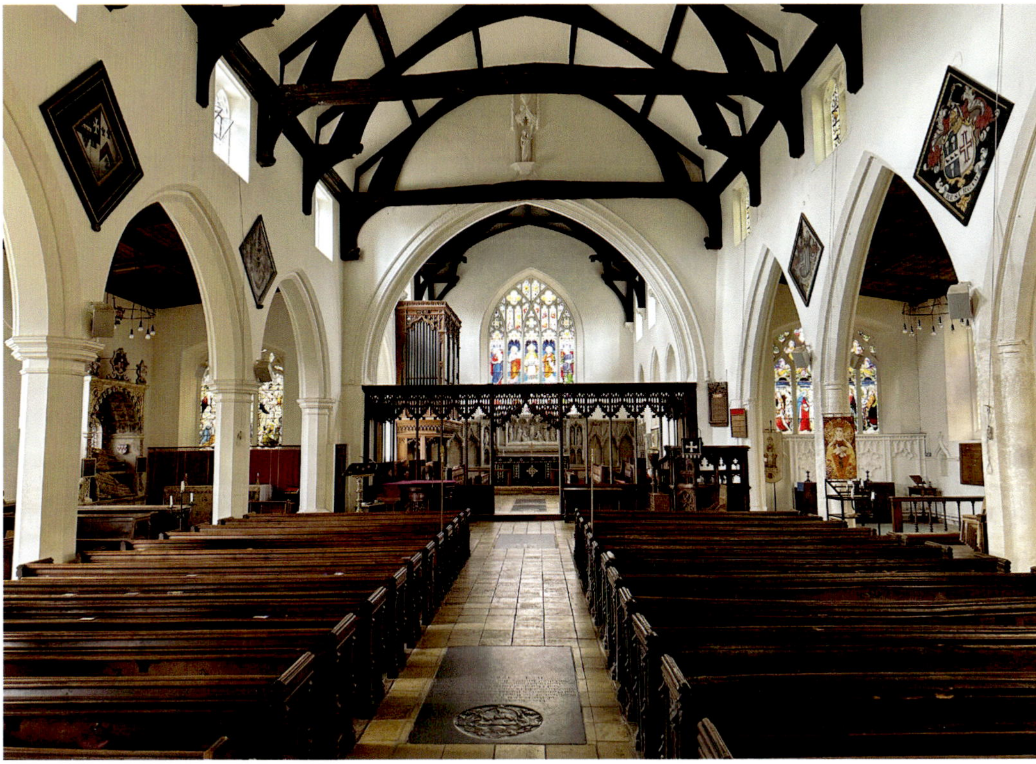

Above: Great Waltham. Interior looking east. The south aisle was added in the fourteenth century and the north aisle in 1875. You can see the monument to Sir Anthony Everard on the left.

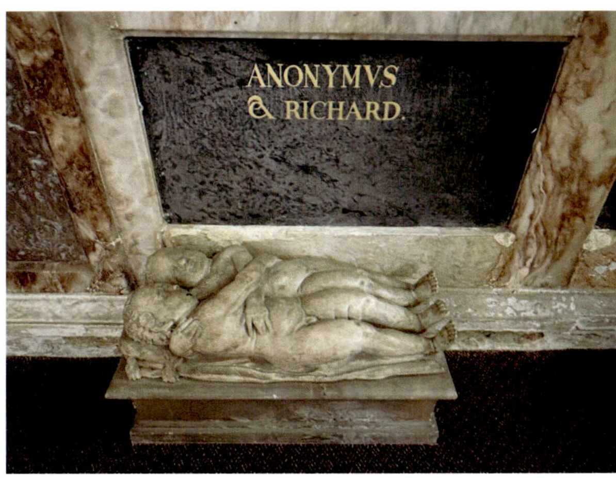

Right: Great Waltham. This sad baby at the base of the monument to Sir Anthony Everard was never named, so is represented by the word 'anonymous'.

25. Great Warley, St Mary the Virgin

For lovers of the Arts and Crafts movement there aren't enough superlatives to describe this church which ranks in the top five of such churches in the country. It was built in 1904 as a memorial to Arnold Heseltine and paid for by his brother. The architect was Charles Harrison Townsend and most of the furnishings are by

William Reynolds-Stephens, both national figures in the world of Arts and Crafts design. The church is approached through a lychgate carved by Eric Gill and you are immediately confronted by the east end of the apsidal, roughcast church. Passing the private door into the pew of the Heseltines, you enter by a porch at the west end of the nave into a rich interior full of sculpture and colour. The nave has aluminium-painted plaster panels reaching up to the roof, wall panelling inset with mother of pearl and original electroliers. The benches are made of walnut. From the nave there are views into the chancel and private pew. The latter became a War Memorial Chapel and is dominated by a marble relief 'The Gateway to Life' which depicts angels watching over the dead Christ. The painted ceiling here is by Reginald Hallward, another Arts and Crafts practitioner of national renown. The chancel screen takes the form of a row of fruit trees and in front of it are lectern and pulpit, the latter with a reading light of translucent glass in the manner of a Tiffany lamp. Up a few steps the chancel contains an organ embellished with copper panels showing scenes from the Benedicite which shimmer in the light and which are supported by a hammered steel frame decorated with square poppies. Astonishingly, the apse ceiling is covered with aluminium leaf, which sets off the altar, which has, as a reredos, a large figure of Christ, his hand raised in blessing. The apse walls are lined with veined marble to create a rich effect and three-dimensional grapes drip down the aluminium vault. Here the windows are by Louis B. Davies, but sadly his other windows designed for the church were

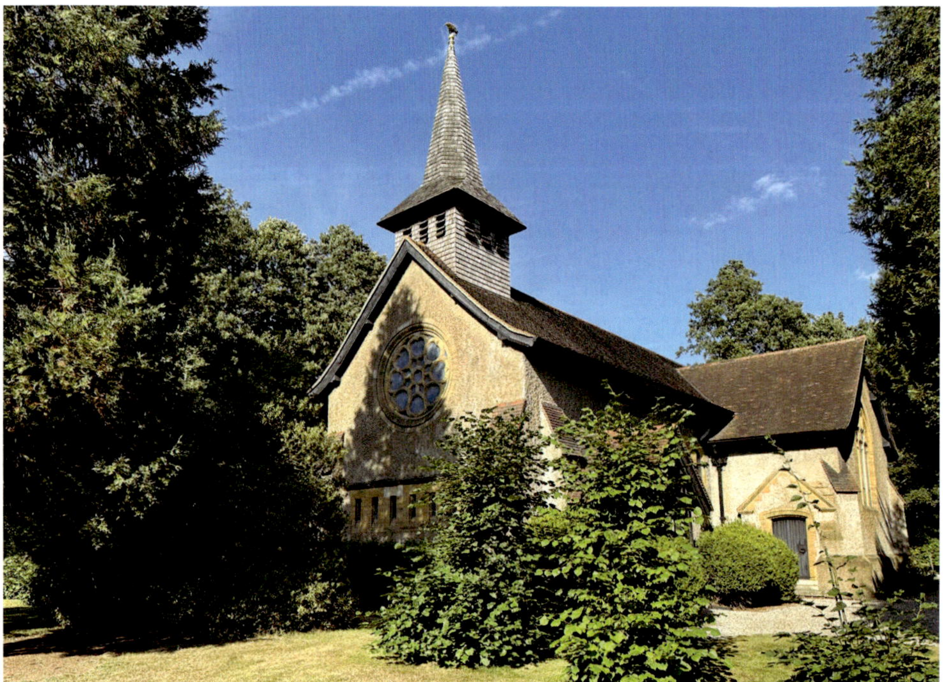

Great Warley. The most important Arts and Crafts building in Essex, built in 1904, viewed from the south-west.

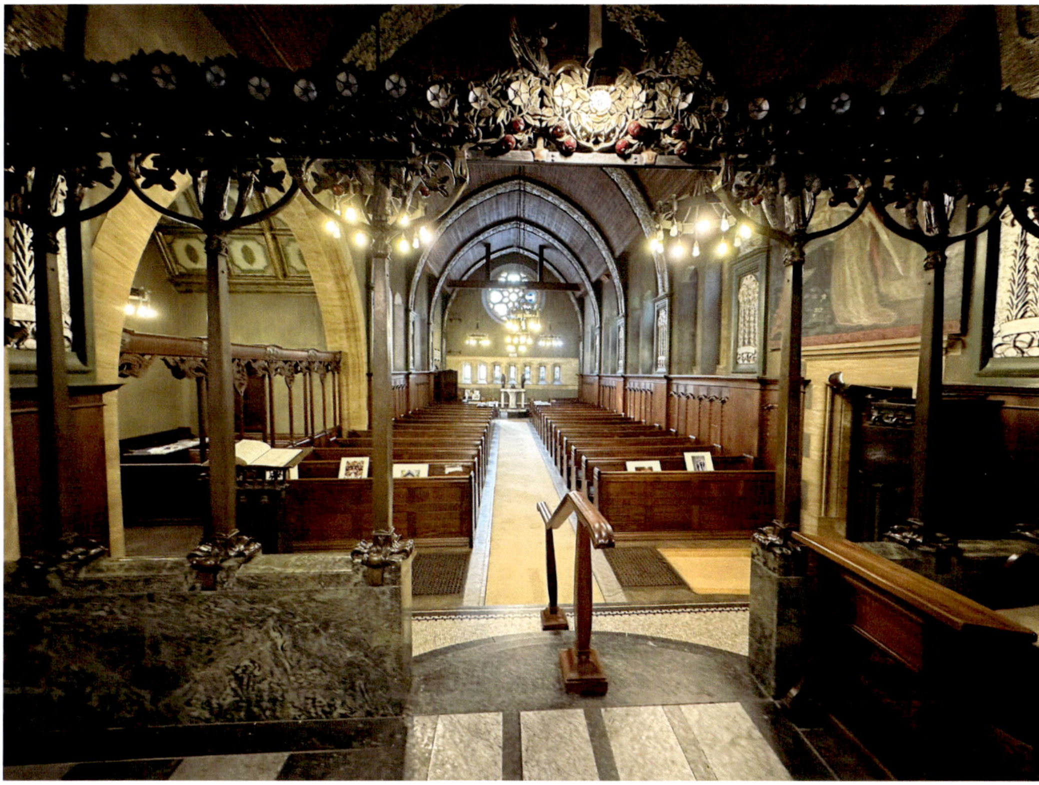

Great Warley. Interior looking west through the screen with mother of pearl inlay. The private pew on the left later became the War Memorial Chapel.

destroyed in the war. At the west end is the font, formed of two marble piers, each of which supports a bronze angel overlooking a bronze and blue mother of pearl cover. This astonishing church is open a few hours each week in the summer or by appointment.

26. Greensted, St Andrew

One of the most famous churches in Britain, bringing thousands of visitors to this little village outside Ongar. They come to visit the oldest surviving wooden building in England. Books will tell you that it is Saxon in date and that here rested St Edmund's body on its journey to Bury St Edmunds in 1013, but we now know that the church is later than that. It may *just* date from the Saxon period, being a year or two before the Norman Conquest (1066), but tree-ring dating suggests an early Norman date is more likely. The nave north and south walls survive from the original building, the chancel being a Tudor rebuild in brick and the white weatherboarded tower an eighteenth-century addition. The church seems much larger outside, for you step into a dark, homely interior with an incredibly low roof structure of the 1890s. This was a time when the legend of St Edmund was popular, so it is not surprising that one of the spandrels in the roof carries a

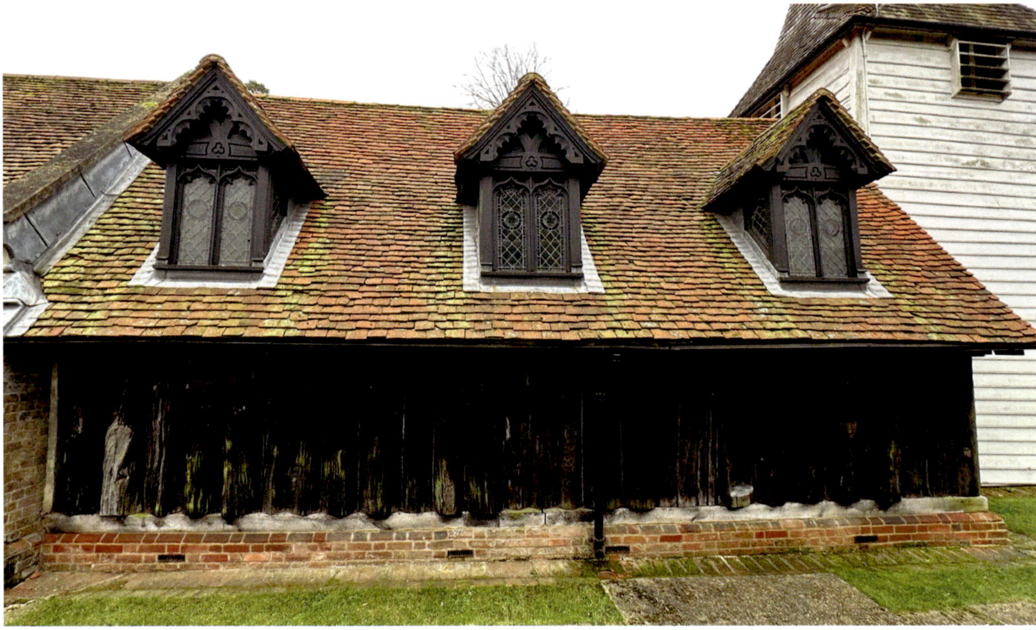

Greensted. The north wall of the nave dates from the eleventh century and is constructed of logs split in half vertically. The dormer windows are Victorian.

depiction of the wolf guarding Edmund's head taken from his legend. A stained-glass window by Lavers, Barraud and Westlake depicts Edmund's martyrdom before he was beheaded. There are few memorials in the church, but the alabaster tablet (1585) to Joan Smith who lived virtuously to the age of sixty-six is worth noting for its very distinctive use of the number five. The wooden font is twentieth century and was designed by president of the Royal Academy, Sir Hugh Casson. The church contains one of those objects very much of its period – a model of the building made of matchsticks. In the days of reduced smoking and electronic lighters, models like these will never again be produced and must be treasured.

27. Hatfield Broad Oak, St Mary the Virgin

A former monastic church, what remains is the nave of a twelfth-century Benedictine priory, rebuilt in the fifteenth century. One of the larger churches in Essex, it is light and airy and contains a host of interesting features. The nave is dominated by an enormous brass chandelier purchased in 1780. It hangs over a set of box pews (1843) with poppy-head finials by Richard Carpenter, the nineteenth-century architect who went on to great things but whose restoration of this church was his first. He incorporated four wooden carved symbols of the Evangelists which had previously been part of an eighteenth-century re-seating. It is the wide selection of monuments that the visitor comes to see. In the centre of the chancel, though not in its original position, is the cross-legged effigy of Robert de Vere, 3rd Earl of Oxford. It is interesting as a piece of historicism as it doesn't date from his time (he died in 1221) but from about 100 years later. At some stage it has been outside

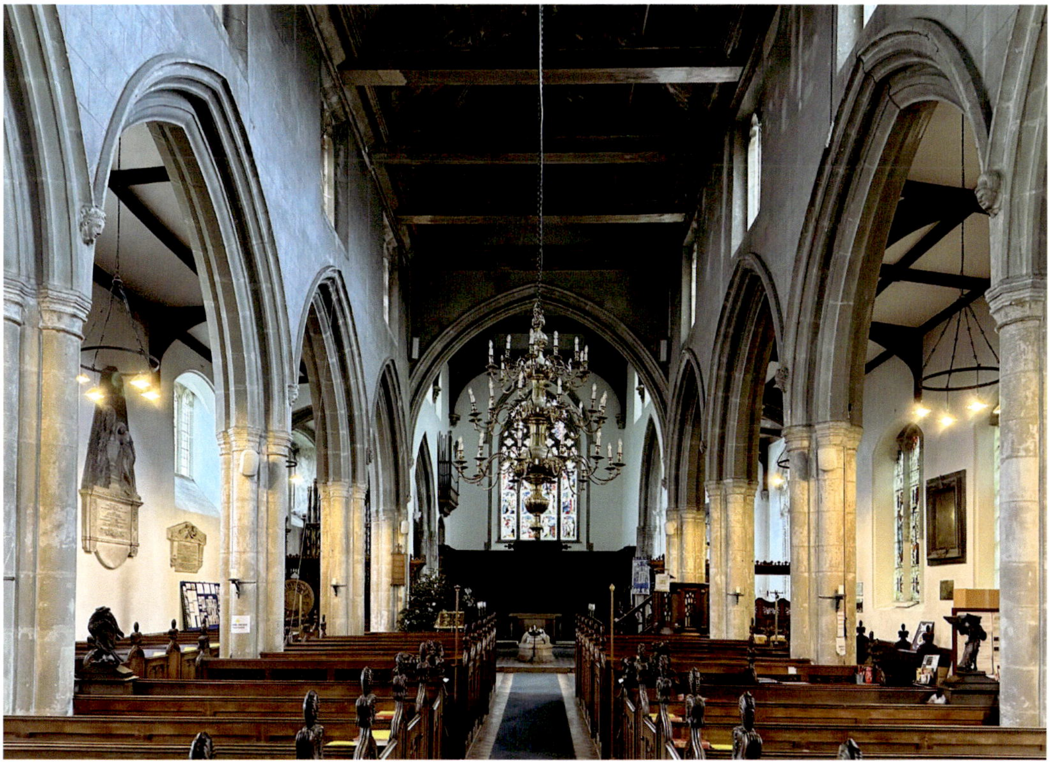

Above: Hatfield Broad Oak. This was once a monastic church. The splendid chandelier dates from 1780.

Right: Hatfield Broad Oak. In the centre of the chancel is the cross-legged effigy of Robert de Vere (d. 1221) made about a hundred years after his death as an act of historicism.

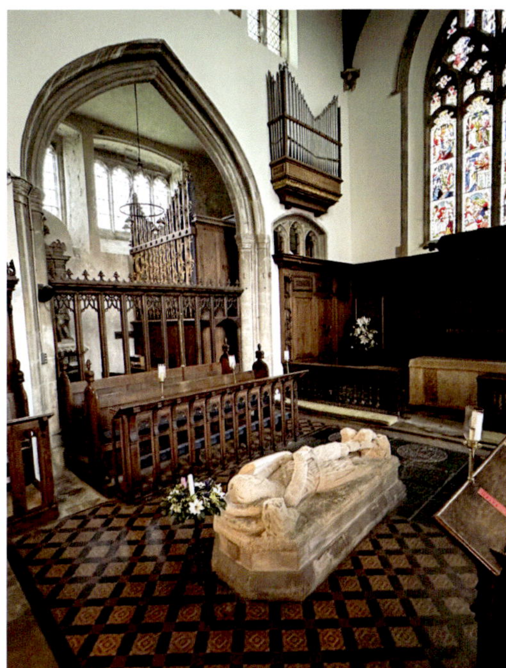

and is in poor condition. The de Vere family had founded the priory, so it is likely that this monument was moved from a more prestigious part of the building at the dissolution of the monastery. Sir John Barrington (died from smallpox in London at the age of twenty-one in 1691) is commemorated by a flaming urn against which lean two distraught putti. It is rumoured to be by Grinling Gibbons. Nearby is a large wall tablet to a later John Barrington, which has an oval portrait of a weeping woman with an urn and above it a sarcophagus bearing his initials. Touchingly, it was erected 'As a tribute of respect for a most sincere friend'. The royal arms are of King George II whilst a large Benefaction Board at the back of the church lists the properties that had been left to provide an income for the poor of the parish.

28. Helions Bumpstead, St Andrew

What a charming and unexpected church this is. As you climb through the churchyard it is immediately obvious that this is going to be an out of the ordinary building, as you are faced with three enormous timber-framed windows which give a domestic feeling, and a red-brick tower. Indeed, this medieval church was so rebuilt in the early nineteenth century that it has a unique Georgian feel. You step into a building where not just the walls and ceilings are light, but the furnishings

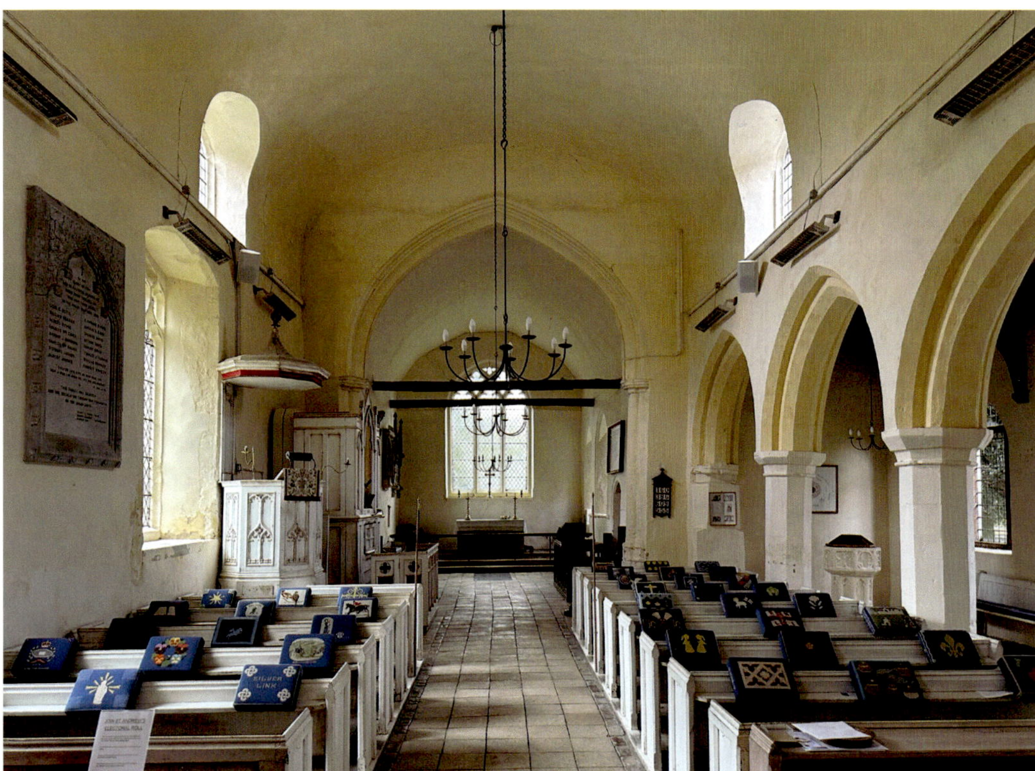

Helions Bumpstead. Interior looking east. The character of this church is given by a mixture of medieval stonework, Georgian rebuilding and twentieth-century furnishing.

too, painted white, the coolness relieved only by a superb selection of hassocks displayed on them. The medieval origins of the church are best seen inside, with traditional windows in the north wall and in the chancel where the priest door has its original drawbar locking system where a pole slides into the wall. The roof is completely coved and ceiled and is lit by dormer windows; in fact, it makes the south aisle feel dark, even with its enormous wooden-framed windows! The furnishings are a wonderful twentieth-century conceit, some made up from wood from the Georgian gallery. The pulpit, with its sounding board, is especially fine and matches the spikey organ next door. The nave has very few memorials, but there are some interesting examples in the chancel. The inscription on a wooden board to William Tabersham (d. 1771) reminds us that in his long life he may not always have been good, but we probably haven't been either, so we should remember his best parts. The ledgerstone to William Sharpe (d. 1692) has some really outlandish spelling, written as it sounded, whilst the colourful Tallakarne monument is supported by two caryatids. The female figure has exposed breasts and one of those rigid Elizabethan hairdos with no hair out of place. Bizarrely, her husband has hairy lips and plucked eyebrows! At the back of the church is an old Bible, showing that the place name was then Bumpsted Helion. As you leave the church look out for the two cast-iron grave markers near the gate.

29. Lambourne, St Mary and All Saints

Few would imagine a rural treasure house like this within the M25. The church stands at the end of a dead-end lane opposite the medieval Lambourne Hall. As the visitor walks up the path, the blocked Romanesque north doorway is obvious to see with its zig-zag carving. There is a less fancy blocked doorway of the same date on the south side too. The church is limewashed to protect its rubble construction and in the south wall of the chancel is a blocked low side window to allow ventilation during the medieval Mass. Today the church is entered from the west, but originally it must have been entered from the north as high on the south wall is a fragmentary image of St Christopher, whose image was always opposite the main doorway. It's a very important piece of late medieval art by an artist of superb ability. The church is packed full of monuments, but before we study these it's worth saying that its medieval structure peers through. Under the gallery of 1726 it is possible to see the vertical supports for the timber belfry with a fictive decorative column visible on the south side. As part of the eighteenth-century remodelling the fourteenth-century crown post of the nave roof was given an extravagant icing of plaster, making it look like a palm tree! The chancel arch is of the same date, topped by a large royal arms and two of the six funeral hatchments to be found in the church belonging to the Lockwood family. It is their monuments that dominate the interior. On the north wall of the chancel is the monument to John Lockwood (d. 1778) which depicts the figure of Hope holding an anchor, leaning nonchalantly on an urn, and a lamp whose flame has gone out. On the south wall is a sculpture by Alfred Gatley, an English sculptor based in Rome, dated 1860, which records the death of Captain George Lockwood during the Charge of the Light Brigade at Balaclava in 1854. The inscription records that his body was never recovered. The regimental flags are laid up, his busby and sword

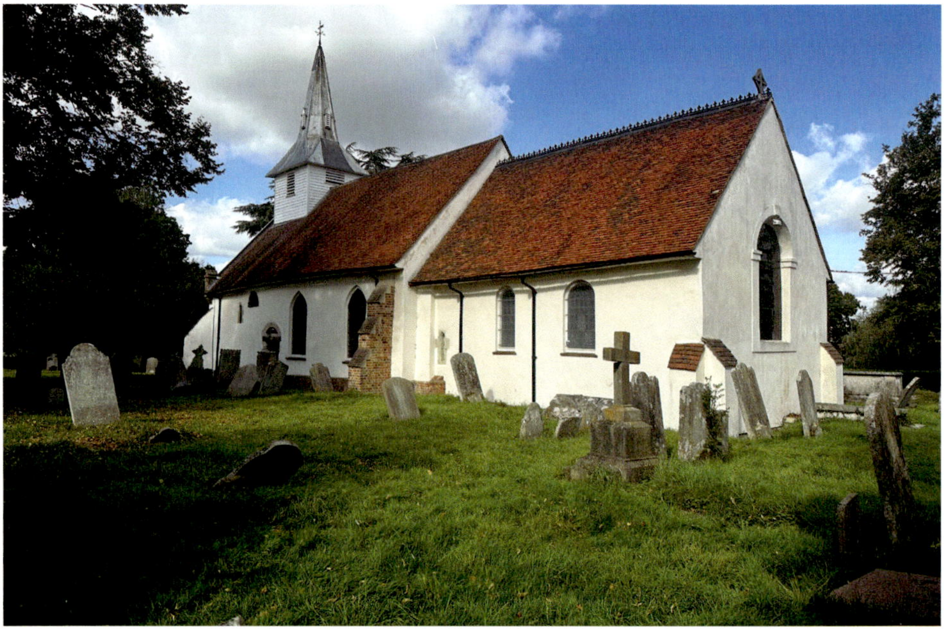

Lambourne. During the medieval period almost every Essex church would have looked like this, with limewash covering the exposed walling to stop it being damaged by the weather.

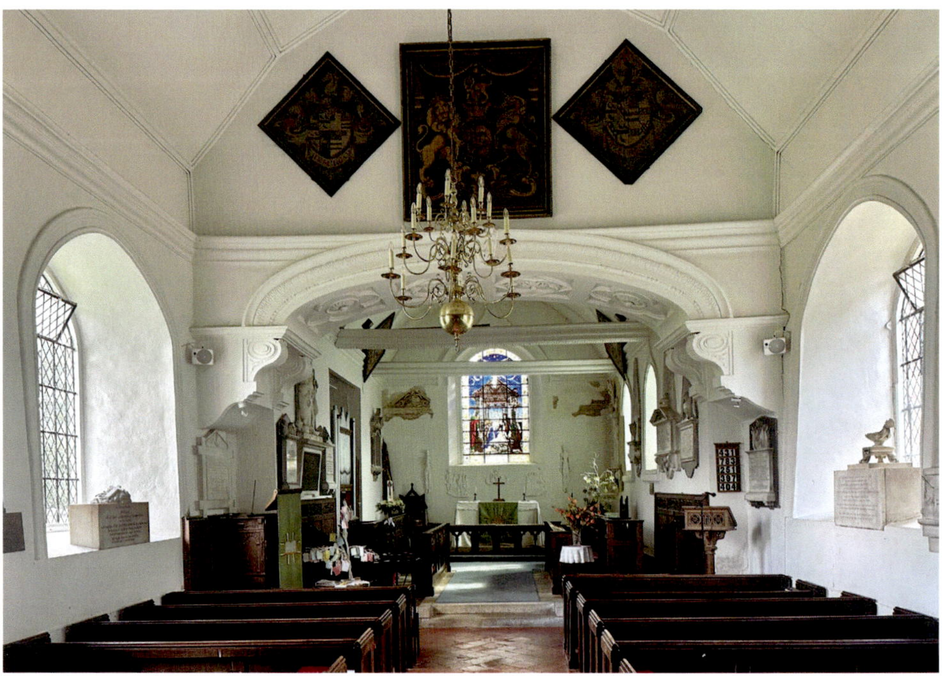

Lambourne. The interior was given a Georgian makeover with prominent plaster decoration, the royal arms over the chancel arch and armorial hatchments.

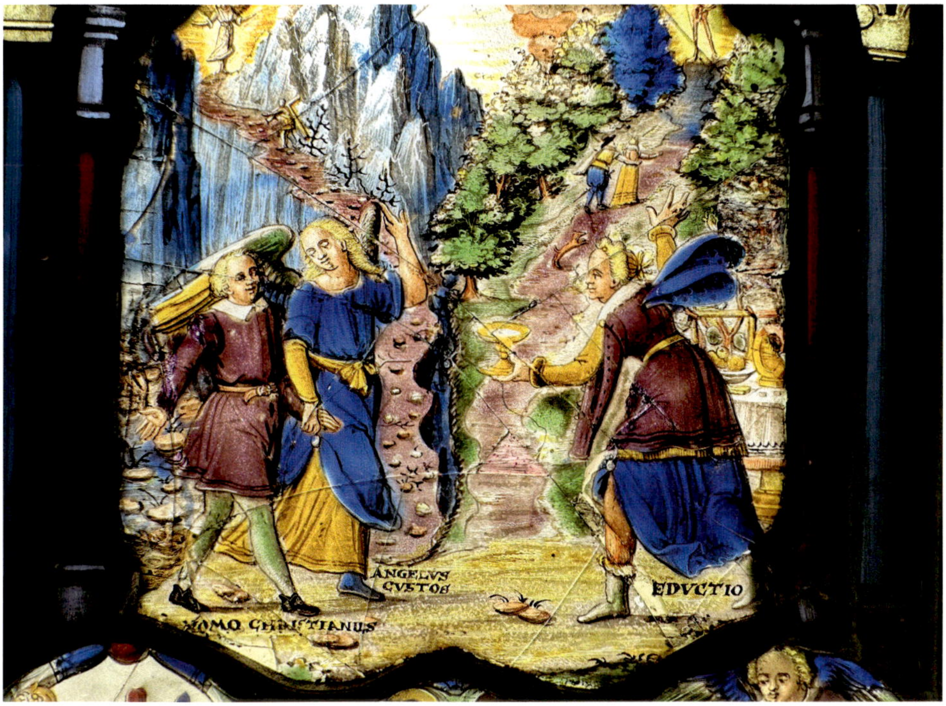

Lambourne. The church has a remarkable collection of seventeenth-century Continental glass. Here a man in green stockings is being shown the way to Heaven by an angel.

are placed on the ground and an angel prepares to blow the last trump. The church contains some good examples of seventeenth-century Swiss glass, installed here in 1817. My favourite panel shows an angel (Angelus Custos) showing a young man (Homo Christianus) with green stockings the way to Heaven, although there are also some more traditional Bible scenes.

30. Layer Marney, St Mary the Virgin

Everyone knows Layer Marney Tower, the tallest Tudor structure in the country, built as a gatehouse to a planned mansion by Henry, the 1st Lord Marney in about 1520. Standing in its shadow is the parish church, also built about the same time, and showing many common features. Like the tower, the church is built of brick and its black diapered pattern shows that this was always supposed to be seen. It is like the contemporary work at Hampton Court Palace, which Lord Marney would have known as a member of the Tudor court. Strangely, other parts of the church were rendered to look like stone – especially the windows, which Marney obviously wanted to look expensive. As soon as the church was completed it was decorated and included a huge wall painting of St Christopher carrying the Christ child across the river, his feet surrounded by a variety of fish. Between the chancel and north chapel is a monument to the 1st Lord Marney, who died in 1523 before either church or mansion were completed. The canopy and

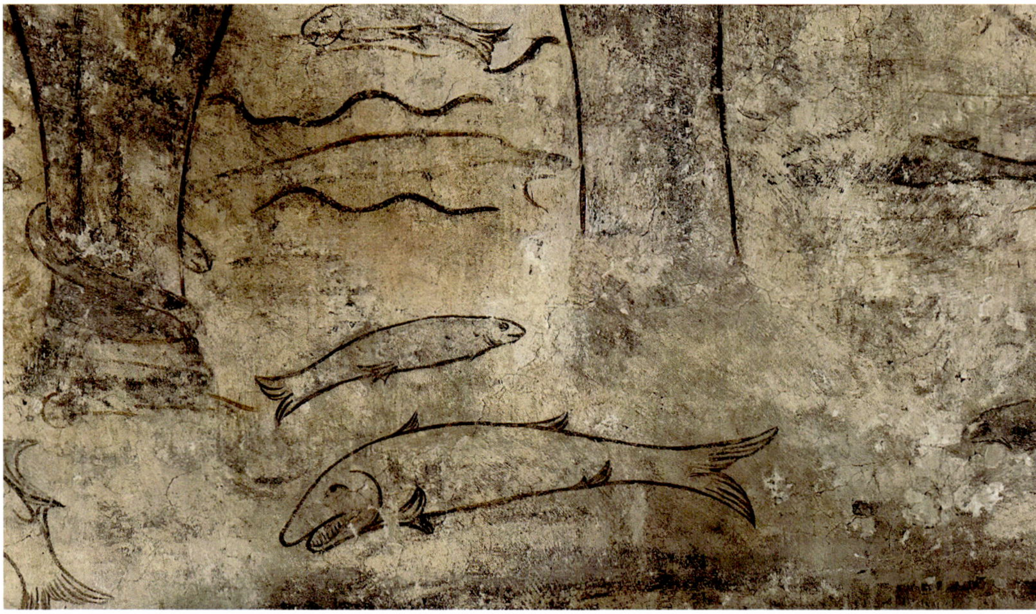

Layer Marney. This sixteenth-century wall painting depicts fish swimming around the feet of St Christopher as he carries the Christ child across a river.

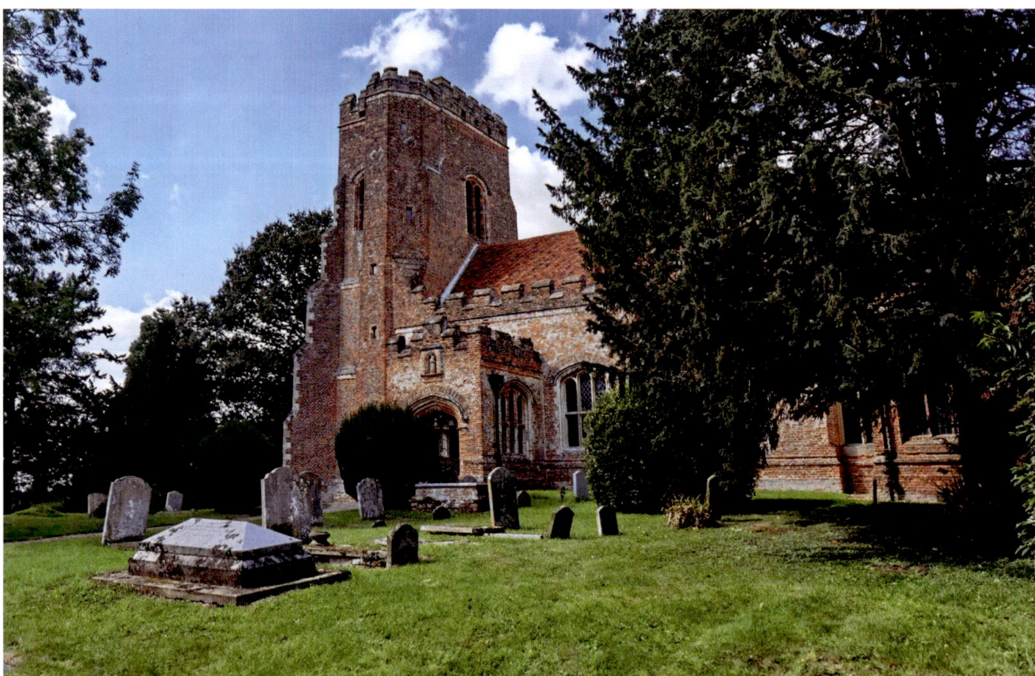

Layer Marney. The church was extensively rebuilt in brick in the early sixteenth century. (Image by Simon Knott)

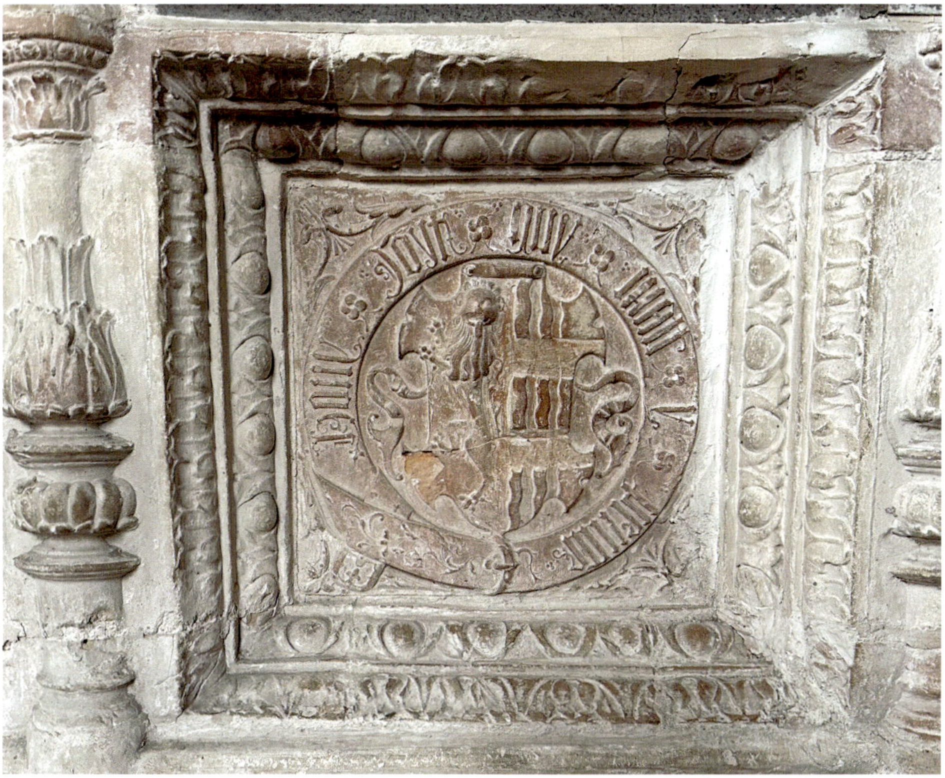

Above: Layer Marney. This terracotta panel forms part of the tomb chest of the 1st Lord Marney, who got the idea of using this cutting-edge material from his position at the Tudor court.

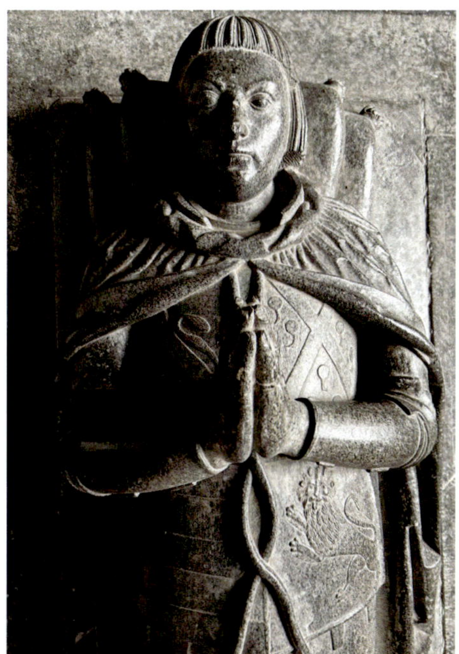

Right: Layer Marney. The effigy in Catacleuse stone of the 2nd Lord Marney, who didn't live long enough to see the mansion started by his father taken to completion.

structure of the tomb is of terracotta, the must-have material for a Tudor courtier, cast in moulds echoing the stone monuments of the time. Marney's effigy is of Catacleuse, a volcanic stone mined in Cornwall and brought around the coast. Essex had no decent stone for carving so this was an excellent choice for a man who could afford anything. Sadly, the Marney heir, Henry's son John, only lived two more years and is buried in the same chapel with a similar monument, but without a canopy. The tomb chest forms a 'T' shape with an altar at which Masses were to be said for the deceased by a priest who lived in a tiny house attached to the north-west corner of the church. The family obviously didn't want for comfort as the north chapel was equipped with an enormous brick fireplace. Nearby is the much earlier tomb of Sir William Marney (d. 1414) which is in alabaster brought from Nottinghamshire. Obviously, the church is all about the Marney family, but it does contain two later items of importance. The first is the south window, which was designed by the famous William de Morgan (1839–1917), lifelong friend of William Morris. As soon as you know that it is by him, the foliage, fruits and flowers of the Arts and Crafts movement jump out at you. The second item is a rare late nineteenth-century figurative memorial brass to a son of the then rector, who died at the age of eighteen in Rio de Janeiro. It shows him kneeling in prayer, having removed his hat, though a friend once remarked to me it looks like he's kneeling in front of the kitchen stove!

31. Lindsell, St Mary the Virgin

One of those churches for visitors who like unusual locations, for St Mary's is accessed through a farmyard and is almost invisible from the road. It's a building of great charm, constructed of flint with red-brick dressings and has attracted artists for many years. In 2005 a linocut of the church by the war artist Edward Bawden sold at Bonhams for nearly £10,000. This is a Norman church that was remodelled in the fourteenth century when the south aisle was added. A huge hagioscope to the right of the Norman chancel arch tells us that there was an altar at this location, the opening giving its priest a view to the main altar. The easternmost arch to the aisle is not fully formed which shows that access from the nave to aisle at this end was important – a fully formed arch would have been a hinderance here because it would be too low. What better way to get round the problem than by letting the arch 'dissolve' into the east wall? In the north wall of the chancel is a shuttered window which communicated with an anchorite's cell. A cell was home to an individual who had decided to retire from the outside world and to live a life of prayer, walled up in a lean-to room. Almost always built like this one on the north side of the chancel they were just large enough for the occupant to lie down. A photograph on display shows the foundations, which were discovered in 1926. The east window contains a fine collection of fragments of medieval glass. In the centre is a pattern of grisaille glass dating from the thirteenth century. This was the medieval equivalent of our frosted glass and let light in without allowing us to be distracted by what was going on outside. There is some fourteenth- and fifteenth-century figurative glass, but the most interesting are two panels that depict donors: Thomas (d. 1514) and Agnes Fytche. If you lift the carpet under the chancel arch you'll find their burial place marked by a

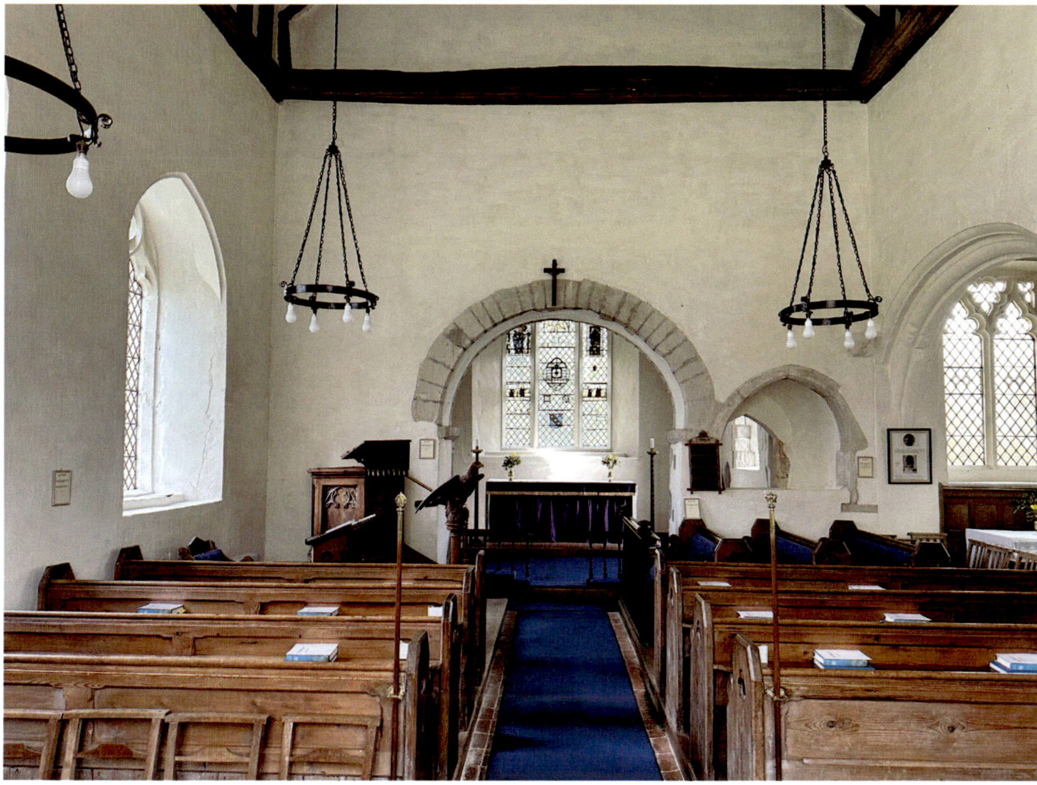

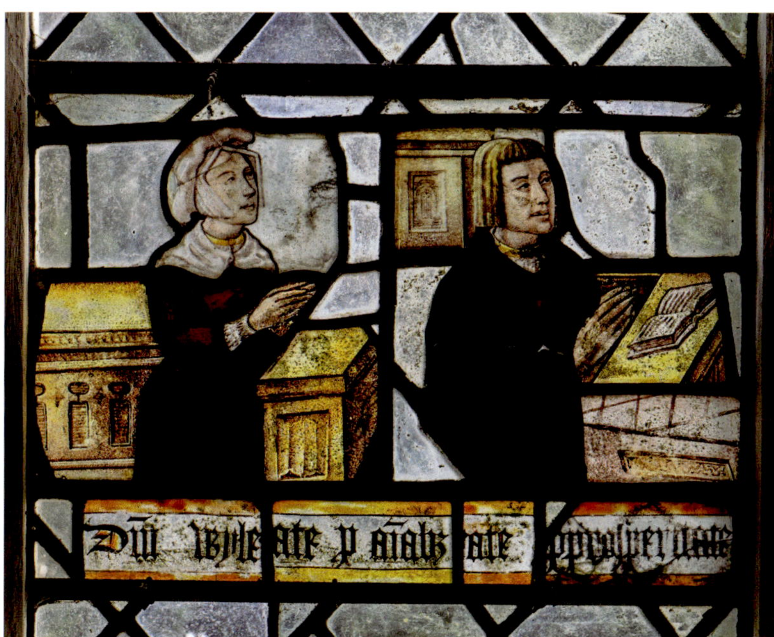

Above: Lindsell. The Norman chancel arch with a later large hagioscope cut through to the right which allowed a priest at a nave altar to see through to the priest at the main altar.

Right: Lindsell. Two donor figures – Thomas and Agnes Fitch – are painted in the east window and should be compared to their effigies in brass by the chancel arch.

brass. By comparing the brass and the window you'll see that brasses were rarely portraits, but bland representations of the type of person commemorated. On the other hand, the painted glass is much more realistic and natural, even though it too may not be an exact depiction of the deceased.

32. Little Braxted, St Nicholas

As you travel around Essex you will frequently come across the name of Revd Ernest Geldart in relation to nineteenth-century restoration works. Not only a clergyman but an artist, craftsman and scholar, Geldart was generous with his talents in assisting incumbents in improving their churches. Little Braxted was his own parish, so we shouldn't be surprised that his artistic eye left a major legacy here. In fact, it is his *magnum opus*. Architecturally, the church is a Norman rectangle with an apsidal east end and a later north aisle, all on a tiny scale. This makes Geldart's contributions even more amazing, for he beautified every internal surface with a dazzling decorative scheme. The walls are covered with a stencilled pattern – green and red in the nave and gold in the chancel. Stencilled inscriptions abound. There are three large paintings, executed on canvas and attached to the walls, the most striking of which is in the north aisle

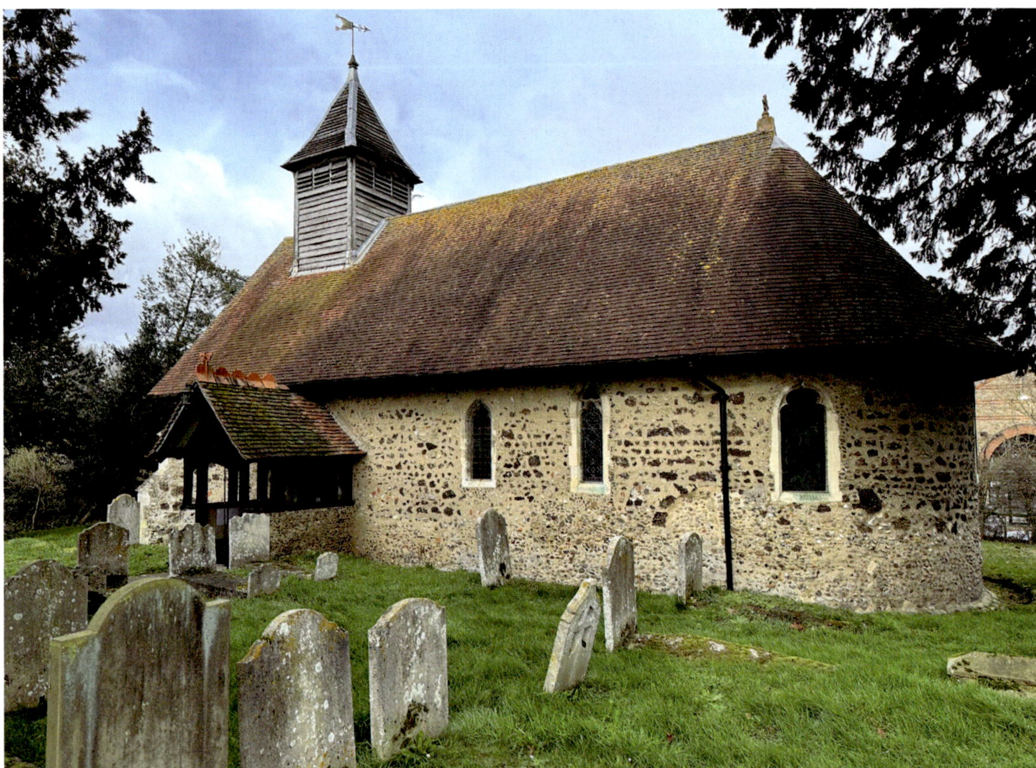

Little Braxted is a diminutive Norman church with an apsidal chancel. Its walls are constructed of flint and puddingstone.

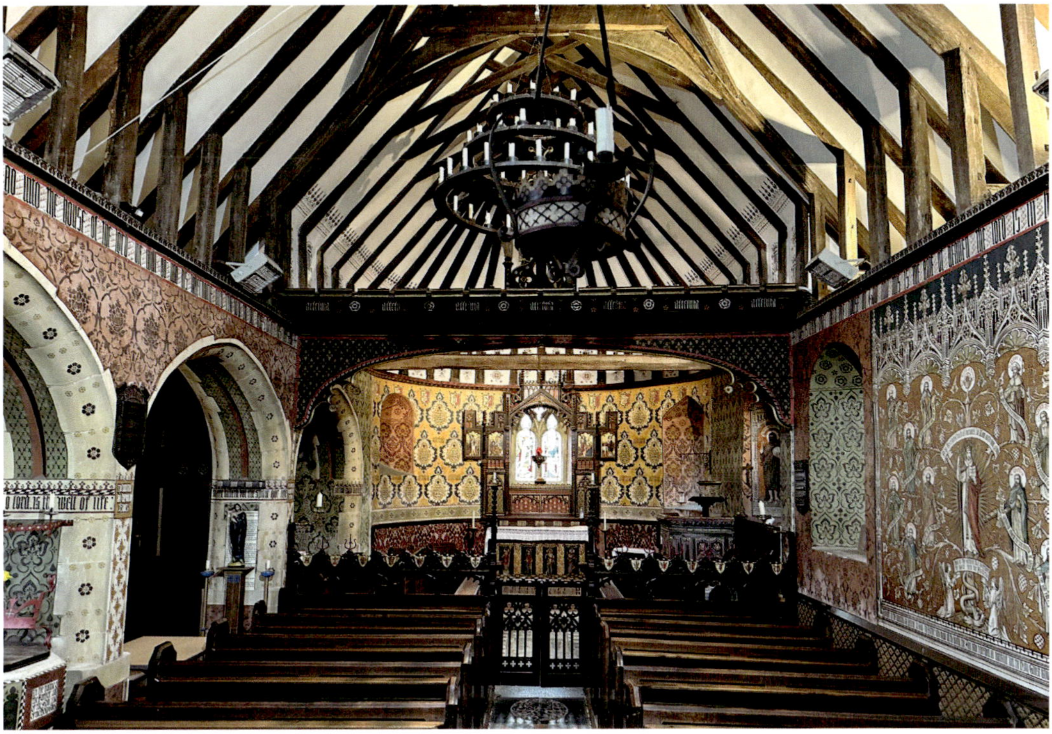

Above: Little Braxted. The interior is the magnum opus of Revd Ernest Geldart, who was incumbent here and who created a mystical, prayerful, interior by the use of applied decoration.

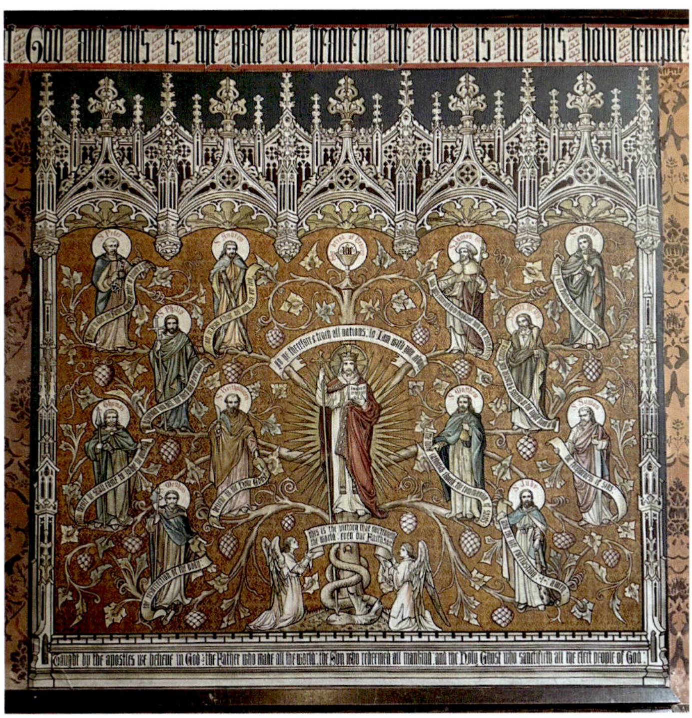

Right: Little Braxted. This painting on canvas by Revd Ernest Geldart depicts Christ and the Twelve Apostles and was stuck to the plaster of the church.

and represents three trees. The dado around the base of the walls is of raffia in the nave and brocade in the chancel. The piscina in the chancel was carved by Geldart and then painted with fictive cusping, and the iron-doored aumbry next to it is painted with fictive arcading. He also designed the stained glass, which was made for him by commercial firms. On the pier separating nave from north aisle is a Latin inscription from the Book of Chronicles which describes the building of the Temple, 'the northernmost pillar of which was called Boaz'. Geldart did likewise. One of the hallmarks of Geldart's work is his use of painted tile inscriptions, and at the west end is a set listing the incumbents of the church since the fourteenth century. Geldart would be delighted to see that it has been kept up to date. Amid this riot of late nineteenth-century design, it is odd to find a rather good memorial brass to William Roberts (d. 1518), his two wives and children in the central gangway.

33. Little Dunmow, St Mary

Essex was once heavily populated by monastic houses, especially those of the Augustinian Order so beloved of King Henry I. One of the royal courtiers, Geoffrey Baynard (of Baynard's Castle in the City of London) founded a priory on his estate here for Augustinian canons in 1106. What survives as the parish church is just the Lady Chapel added onto the priory in the late thirteenth century. It is a magnificent building. The blocked arcade that once led into the priory is formed of chunky piers, made all the more impressive by being preserved intact rather than being walled in as is usually the case. The south wall is a treasure trove of naturalistic carving, the blank arcade having dozens of creatures carved into its spandrels. You'll find all manner of creatures both real and imagined, but my favourite has to be the man stroking a cat which is biting his tunic. Traces of colour survive to show how glorious this must have once looked. More colour survives in the fourteenth-century tiles that have been grouped together near the altar rails. If the priory was floored throughout by similar tiles it must have been a wonderful sight. Look for the couple holding hands and for the lion rampant guardant (two front feet off the floor and looking out). Close by is the famous Flitch Chair, formerly used in the ceremony of the Dunmow Flitch. Of particular interest are three monuments. Two are medieval and of alabaster. The one with two effigies commemorates Walter and Elizabeth Fitzwalter (d. 1432). I love the scribe on the east end holding a tablet and two quills; I'm sure not many people notice him. In the central gangway is a ledgerstone that commemorates John Wylde, whose lawyer father sent him here during the great plague in London. Sadly, he brought the plague with him and died at the age of nine months. To the north of the altar is the large eighteenth-century monument to Sir James Hallet and his family. He is depicted on a portrait medallion held by a disconsolate woman and shows him with a long flowing wig. This medallion is typical of the work of the sculptor Thomas Adye, who worked from about 1730–50 and always signed his work around the rim of these medallions. Hallett had made a fortune as a goldsmith in London; the house created out of the former priory at Little Dunmow was his country seat.

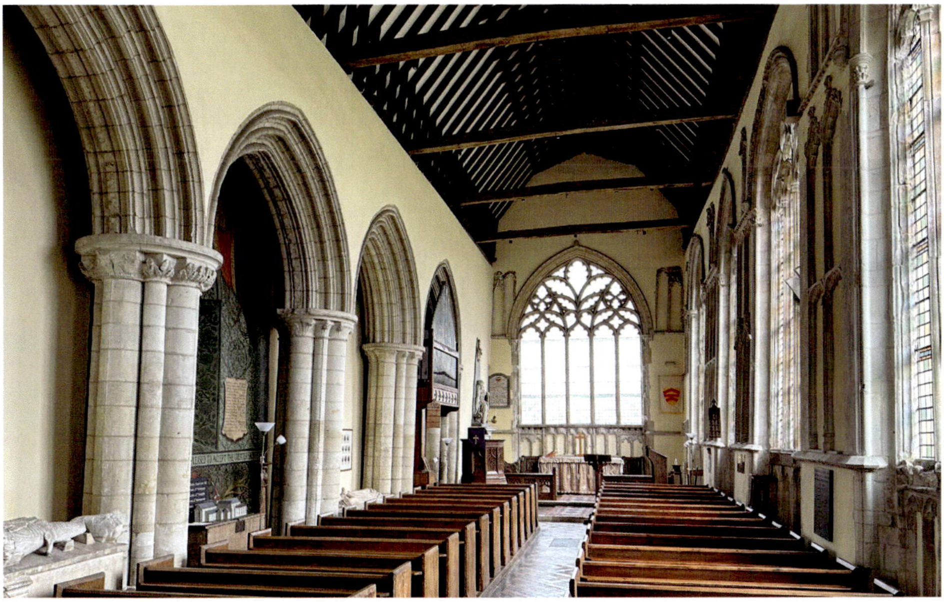

Little Dunmow. This was the Lady Chapel of the Augustinian monastery. Luckily the arcades on the left were preserved intact, rather than being completely infilled.

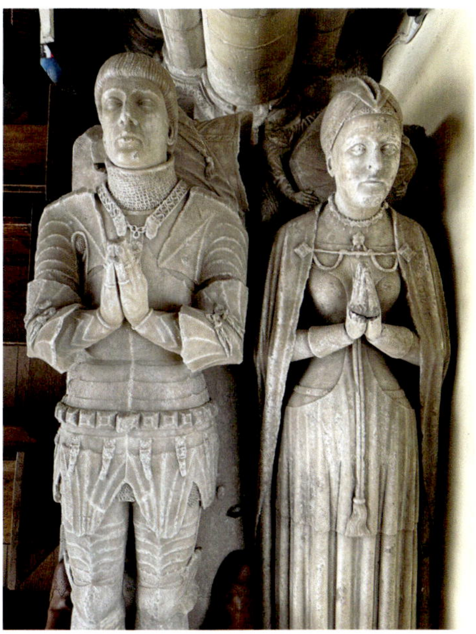

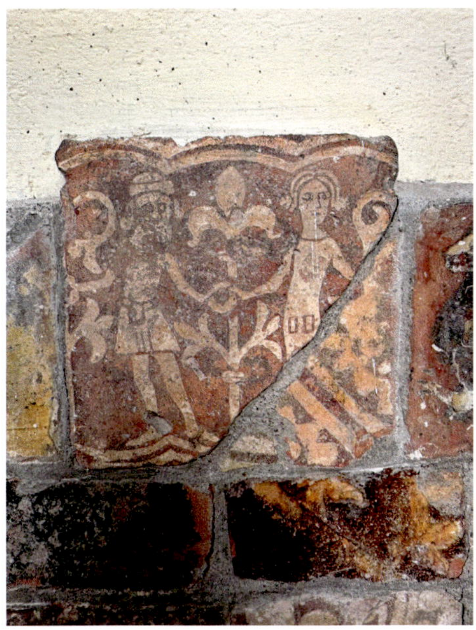

Above left: Little Dunmow. This fifteenth-century monument is carved in alabaster and depicts Elizabeth and Walter Fitzwalter. It would originally have been painted.

Above right: Little Dunmow. This delightful tile showing a couple holding hands would have been on the floor in the original monastery. It probably represents donors.

34. Little Easton, St Mary

A church that would set even the most hardened church crawler's heart a-flutter, St Mary's is very much an estate church, the contents of which reflect the story of the Maynard family. When you enter via the west door the visitor might be forgiven for wondering what the fuss is all about. It looks to be a long simple church with little of interest. Yet as you walk down the nave its treasures reveal themselves with great rapidity. Firstly, on the north wall is the fragment of a very early wall painting, depicting a saint and dating from the twelfth century. He is in a 'man-spreading' pose, holding a book in his left hand and gesturing with his right, and the naïve style is typical of this early period. A watercolour hanging below makes it easier to pick out the detail and is by Professor Tristram, the great twentieth-century expert on medieval paintings. On the opposite side of the church, on the south side, is a much larger and later wall painting showing scenes from the Passion in two tiers. By now the other glories of the interior will have come into view. To the north of the altar is a tall, early fifteenth-century monument to a member of the Bourchier family, original owners of the estate. The striking carved heraldry, now sadly without its original colour, includes the frequent use of water carriers (bougets). The tiny medieval effigy on the tomb

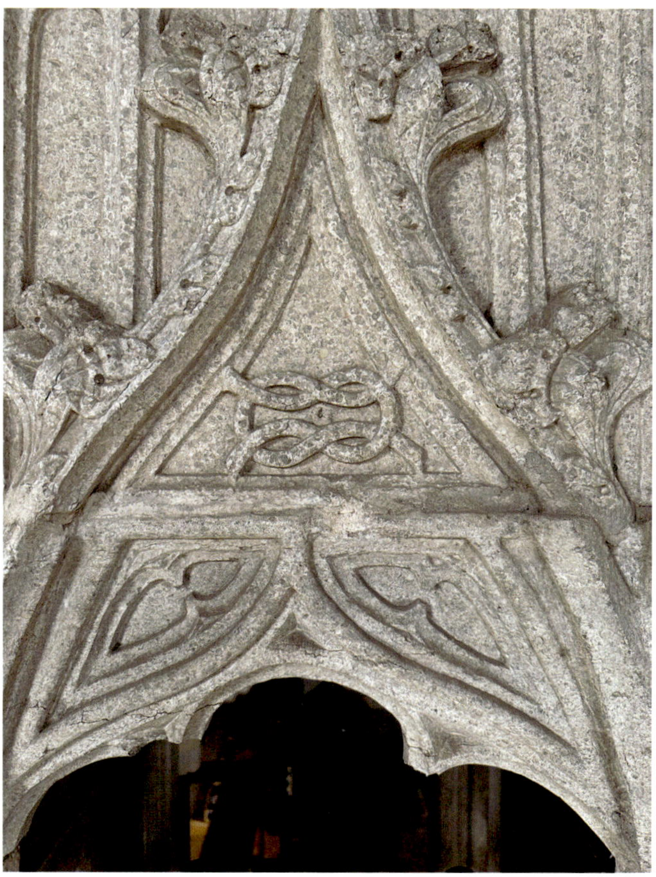

Little Easton. This detail from the Bourchier monument shows the heraldic knot which they used on their shield of arms.

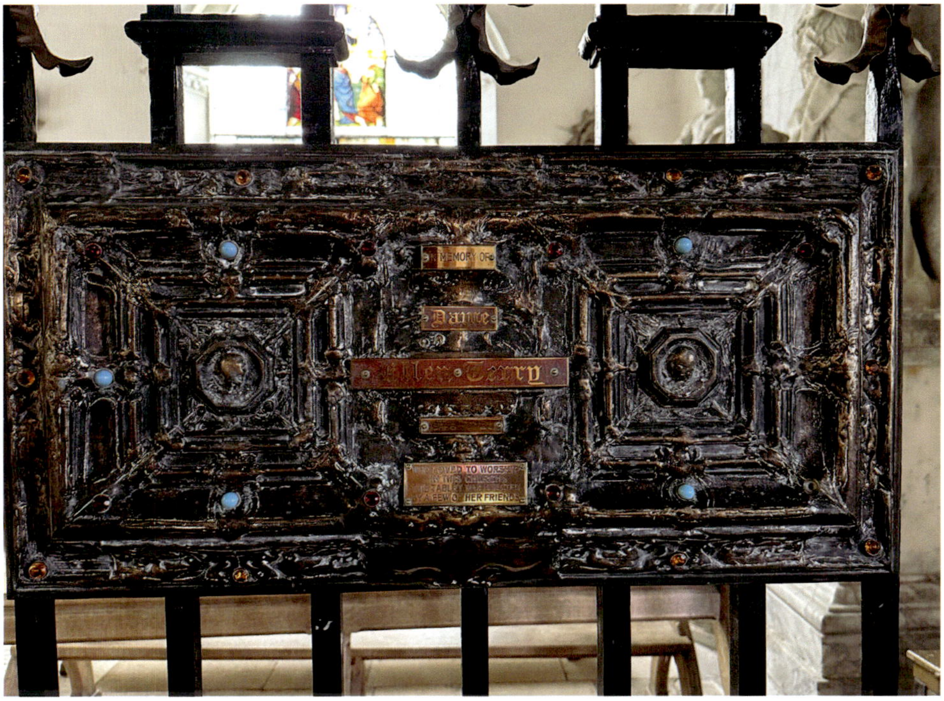

Above: Little Easton. This striking memorial to actress Dame Ellen Terry, a friend of Daisy, Countess of Warwick, was designed by Sir Alfred Gilbert.

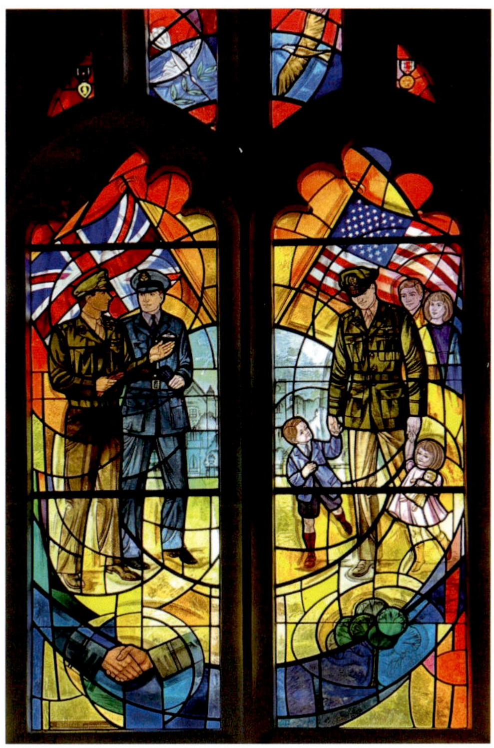

Right: Little Easton. This is one of two windows which commemorate the USAAF Bomb Group who were based here during the Second World War.

chest is nothing to do with the monument and is 200 years earlier. On the right of the chancel is another large monument with a brass on the flat surface. This commemorates Viscount Bourchier (d. 1483) and his wife and was brought from Beeleigh Abbey when it closed. The stonework here depicts another emblem of the Bourchier family, the famous Bourchier Knot. Pass through the iron railings (with superb grotesque faces on the lock) into the Maynard Chapel. This family followed the Bourchiers as owners of the estate and took advantage of the huge chapel they inherited in which to display their monuments. Each monument is worthy of detailed study. In the corner, above the hefty radiator that gave the Maynards some degree of comfort when sitting in their private pew, is a bust of Daisy, Countess of Warwick (d. 1938), courtesan of Edward VII and lady of the manor, whose good works are legendary. Popular tradition asserts that she was the inspiration for the song 'Daisy Bell'. One of her friends was the actress Ellen Terry (d. 1928) who she commemorated by a bronze panel designed by Sir Alfred Gilbert which is now fixed to the chapel railings. On the other side of the church is a memorial chapel to commemorate the USAAF Bomb Group whose base was at Easton Lodge. Two striking windows by the American Phillips Stained Glass Studio record their time here.

35. Little Maplestead, St John the Baptist

One of the most famous churches in England, St John's is one of just five churches in the country to have a circular nave. All took their inspiration from the Church of the Holy Sepulchre in Jerusalem, popularised throughout Europe as a result of the Crusades. Most were built by organisations associated with crusaders, be they the Knights Templar or the Knights Hospitaller, and it was the latter who owned a preceptory here – one of seventy-six properties in England. Although they had owned the property since 1185, the present church was only built in the fourteenth century and, apart from its unusual shape, it contains all the architecture found in a more usual church of the period. The picturesque view from the south is given interest by the tiny gable windows and timber-framed turret and it is clear to see that the chancel is completely run of the mill. Once inside, we find that in fact the nave is hexagonal; only the outer walls of its aisle are circular, the arcades of a common fourteenth-century design. It's rather a pity that the interior is set up with chairs facing east as they somehow fight with the architecture, and it would be easier to understand the building if the nave was kept clear. It contains an interesting font of Norman date, so it predates the present church, and has some rather crude foliate designs carved into the bowl. When the new church was constructed, the font was brought up to date by cutting each of its corners off making it octagonal, which was all the rage at the time. Hence it has four carved sides and four totally plain. The base was completely new. There is a delightful, illuminated roll of honour recalling the villagers who served in the First World War with a little picture of the church incorporated in it, whilst the only other furnishing of note are the Ten Commandments, which date from the early nineteenth century. Nearly everything else is Victorian and dates from the restoration of the 1850s, including the pretty painted ceiling of the chancel and apse.

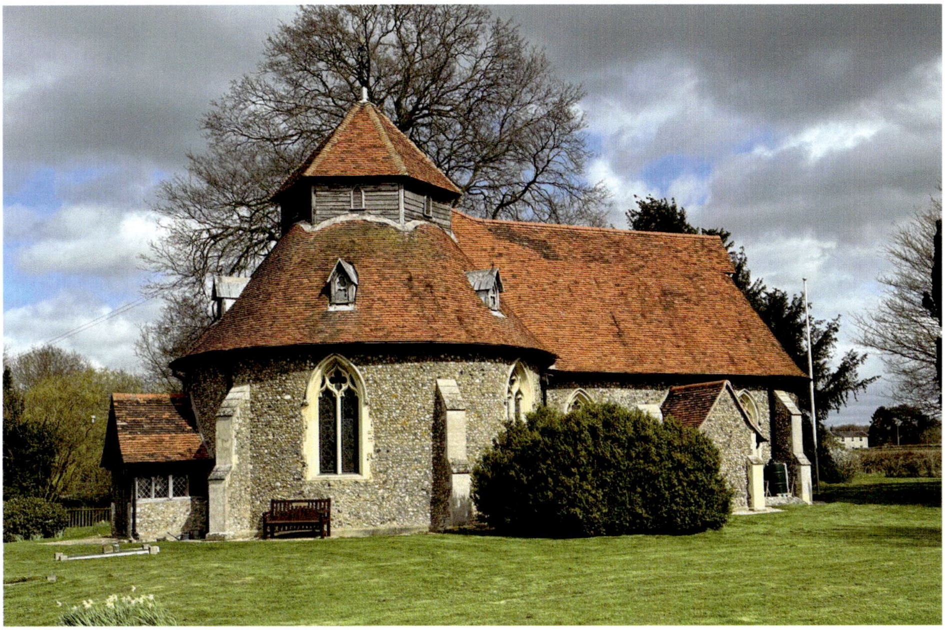

Little Maplestead. One of just a handful of round churches in England, all of which take their inspiration from the Church of the Holy Sepulchre in Jerusalem.

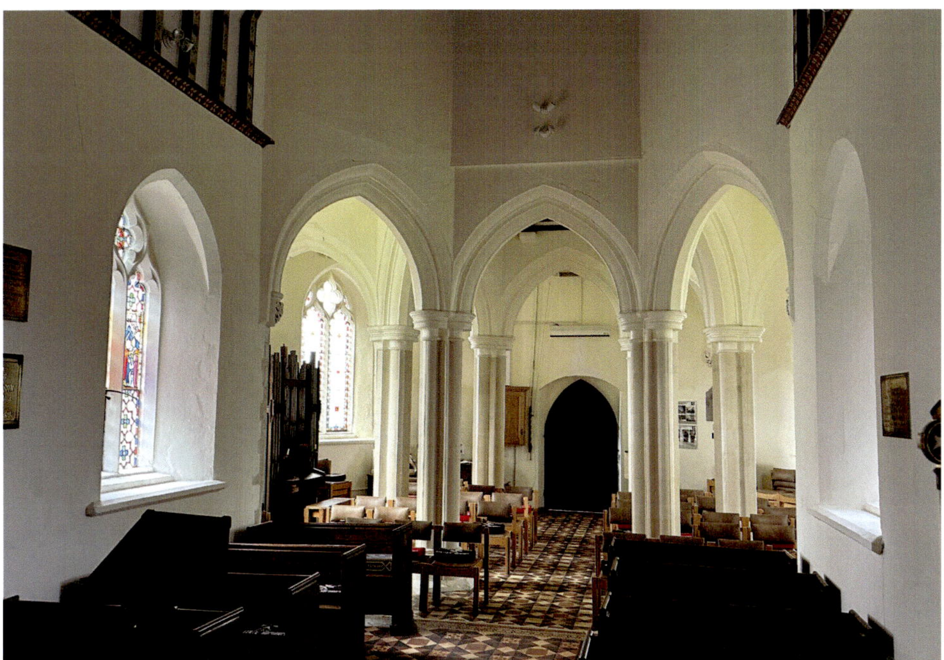

Little Maplestead. Looking from the chancel into the hexagonal nave which in turn stands within a circular outer wall. Almost everything in this photograph is nineteenth century.

36. Mundon, St Mary

This charming church takes a little finding, but it well rewards those who persevere. One of the county's retired churches, it is now in the care of the Friends of Friendless Churches charity. Electricity hasn't yet reached the church, so visit on a bright day to appreciate its rustic interior! The chunky wooden bellcote is supported internally by wooden aisles which are tiled with lean-to roofs which gives the church a witch-hat-like appearance. You enter the base of the tower, where it is easy to see that the aisles are completely useless as spaces. They are just there to hold the weight above and to spread the load on the soft clay ground. From here the view into the church is one of simplicity, with Georgian box pews and clear glass. This is a church that shows modest repairs undertaken over many hundreds of years and where money was never available to wholeheartedly restore. Thank goodness, for it shows us how most of our rural churches must have looked before the Victorians repaired everything in sight. The rough walls tell us that this is the original medieval plaster and, as if to prove it, tiny details of medieval wall paintings peep through here and there. Near the north door you can see two heads, one of which wears a crown, so this is an image of East Anglian St Edmund. It is painted over a pattern of red lines designed to look like stone ashlar, which is always thirteenth century, so Edmund

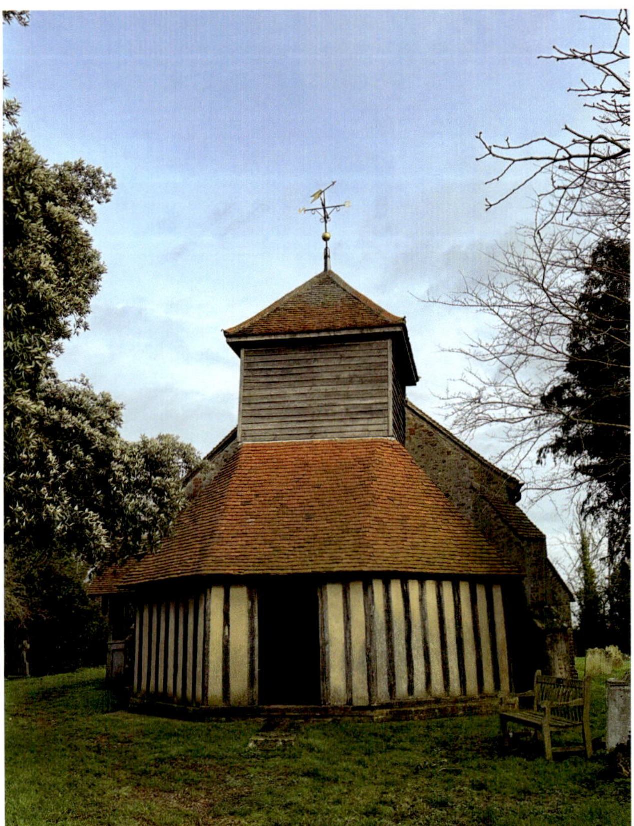

Mundon. This isolated church is entered through the base of a late medieval skirted wooden bell frame.

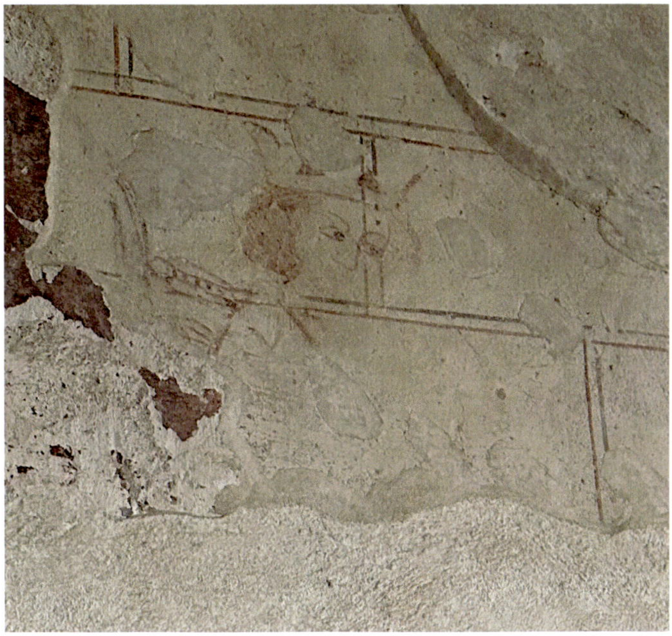

Mundon. This recently discovered wall painting depicts the crowned head of St Edmund, king and martyr, painted over the straight lines of thirteenth-century fictive masonry.

must be slightly later. Elsewhere in the church are more recent wall paintings; for example, the Georgian Lord's Prayer to the north of the Communion table. Once your eyes have adjusted to the glare coming through the east window you'll see that the east wall is entirely painted with fictive curtains, with tassels hanging down towards the Ten Commandments, displayed as required by law at the time. If you go outside you'll find that the chancel is entirely eighteenth century and built of brick. This is due to structural movement which is still a major issue today as the Essex clay expands and contracts depending on how much water is in the soil. The wooden porch on the north side of the church has some delicately carved woodwork in its spandrels. In an isolated location like this, everything possible got recycled.

37. Navestock, St Thomas the Apostle

Serving a scattered population, this church seems remote until you realise it is adjacent to one of the large medieval houses of the parish. Its memorable feature is the fourteenth-century timber-framed skirted bell tower capped by a needle-like spire. Unfortunately, the casual visitor can't gain access to the tower, but the skirt hides a frame that supports the six bells, the earliest of which dates from 1470 (see 36. Mundon for an accessible, though much smaller, skirted tower). The timber theme continues inside the church where it may be seen that the arcade between nave and south aisle is made of timber and covered with plaster. The easternmost arches have been exposed, showing the skeletal construction beneath. It made sense to use the cheapest local materials. The church is ceiled, which gives it a domestic and light-filled interior. The north wall is the earliest part of the church The arch of a blocked Norman window hovers above a later blocked arch that

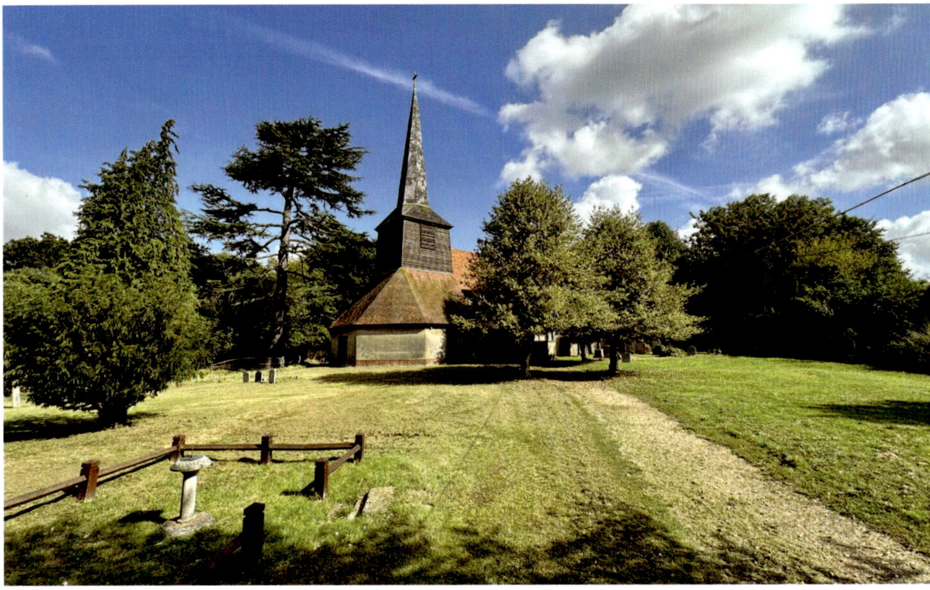

Navestock. Here the wooden bell frame has been continued up to form a tower with shingled spire.

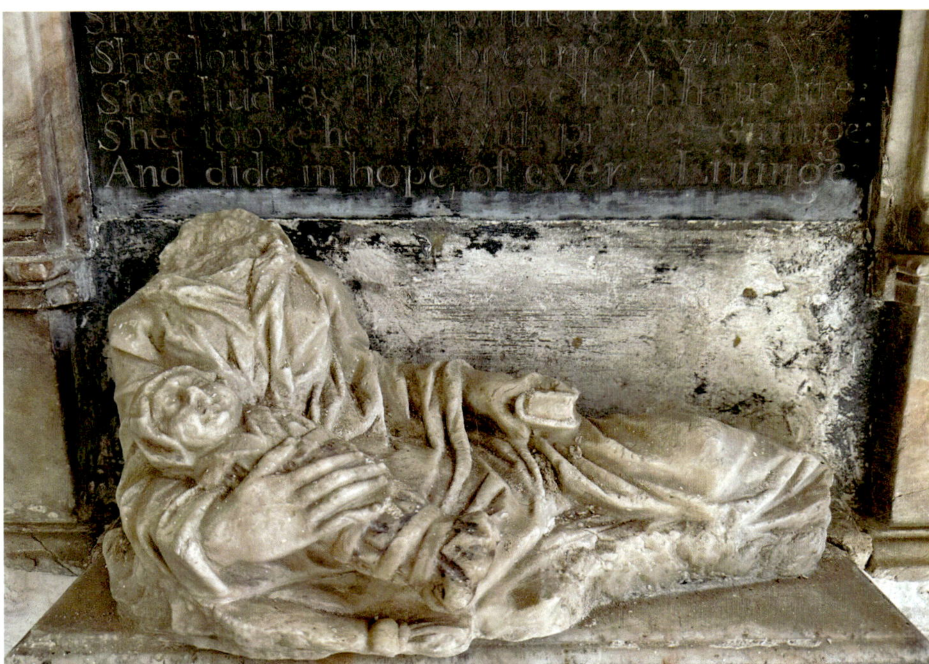

Navestock. The sadly damaged miniature effigy of Ann Snelling and her baby who both died in 1625. Ann died in childbirth and her son shortly afterwards.

once led into a north chapel, and there is a blocked Norman doorway. The church is full of notable monuments, the earliest of which are the two stone coffin lids, now set against the wall by the font, which date from the thirteenth century, each of which is inscribed with a bottonee cross. There are plenty of brass inscriptions set into the floor, but the best is now on the east wall of the church. It remembers Agnes Shounke, née Colford, who died in 1589 and whose inscription is a veritable biography reminding us that she lies here with 'clods of claye'. On the opposite side of the altar is the magnificently coloured memorial to Judge John Greene, dressed in his red robes and holding a scroll with his hand on a book and skull. Heraldry abounds. Greene kept a diary, which gives us useful clues as to the political state of England in the 1650s. Also in the chancel is the sadly damaged monument to Ann Snelling, who died in childbirth in 1625. She is shown as a miniature figure holding her dead baby and a Bible with an explanatory inscription behind. There are two portrait busts of note: Lord Chewton, who was killed at the Battle of Alma in 1854, is depicted by sculptor Matthew Noble whilst the memorial to Lord Radstock was an early work of the sculptor William Behnes (Sculptor in Ordinary to Queen Victoria) and shows the old Admiral 'warts and all'.

38. Pentlow, St Gregory and St George

There are just six churches in Essex that have round towers but there must have once been many more. Round towers were a fashion in the medieval period, built throughout East Anglia and occasionally further afield, all probably taking their inspiration from similar towers in northern Europe. We used to think they were defensive, or designed because there was no good local stone to build corners, but we now know that this cannot be the case. Nor are they all of Saxon date – in fact the majority were built after the Norman Conquest, as is the case here. Here it is one of the more recent parts of the church for the nave with its apsidal chancel is early Norman, and the tower probably thirteenth or fourteenth century. The only later part of the church is a north chapel, which was added in the early seventeenth century to take the magnificent tomb of George Kempe and his family. Three effigies sit on graduated levels, with George on a higher level than his son and daughter-in-law. The two men enjoy red cushions at their head, but poor Elinore has to make do with a black one. The paint is not original, having been repainted in the nineteenth century following the original scheme. A pious individual scratched religious inscriptions into the soft alabaster tomb chest very soon after its installation, possibly during the Commonwealth period. At the base, ten daughters and four sons kneel in silent prayer. The chapel has a splendid plaster ceiling similar to those being installed in houses in the Jacobean period, whilst the east window of the chapel has a fine display of Georgian stained glass – mostly orange and purple – in its tracery. Also in the chapel is the most recent funeral hatchment to have been installed in an English church, commemorating Clifford Stuchfield who died in 2017. On the south side of the chancel is a window depicting the two patron saints of the church, designed by A. K. Nicholson in 1927. Below St Gregory is an interesting depiction of the Anglo-Saxon slaves in the Rome marketplace, which inspired Pope Gregory to send Augustine on his missionary expedition to Britain. Between the chancel and chapel is a plain tomb chest with detailed heraldry on the side showing the arms of the Tudor Felton family. At the rear of the church the Norman font has unusual decorative designs and is topped by a fifteenth-century cover. Nearby is a memorial to the men of the Home Guard in the Second World War. Before you leave, go round the outside of the church where you'll find a Victorian privy – installing facilities in churches is nothing new!

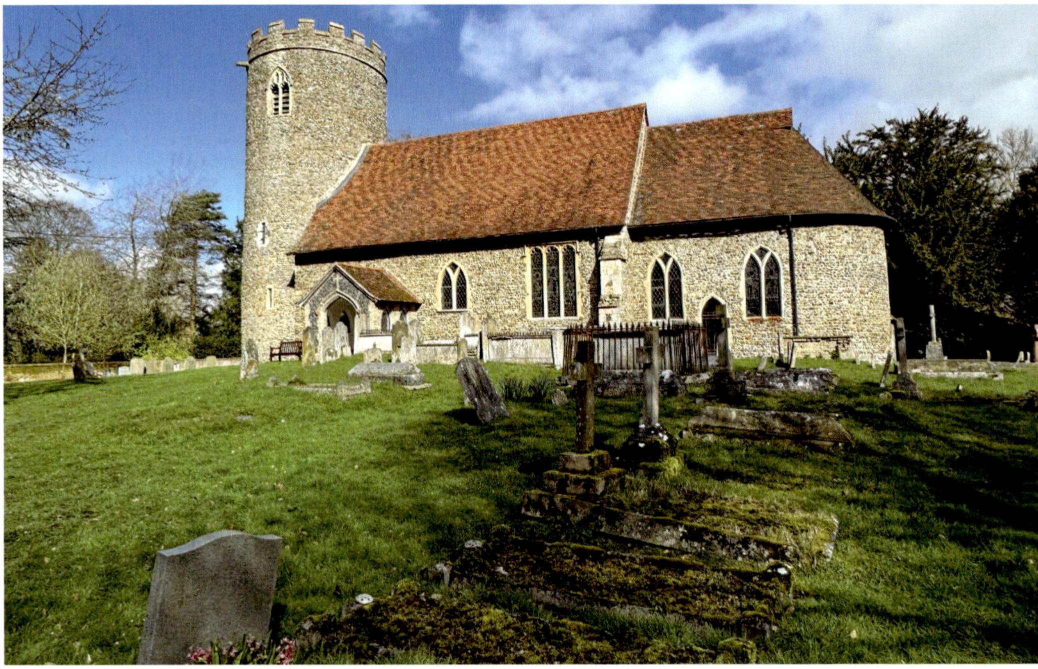

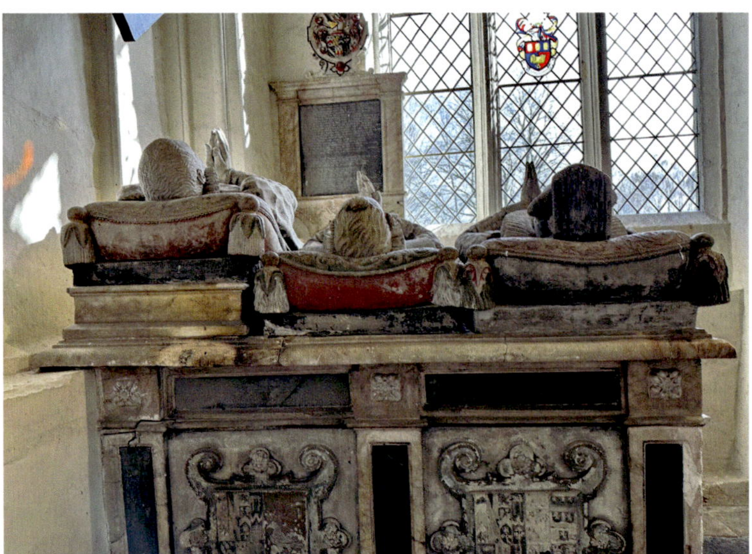

Above: Pentlow. Right on the Suffolk border, this is one of just six round-towered churches to survive in Essex. The church also has an apsidal chancel.

Left: Pentlow. This monument shows Judge George Kempe, who died 1606, along with his son John and daughter-in-law Elinore, who both died in 1609.

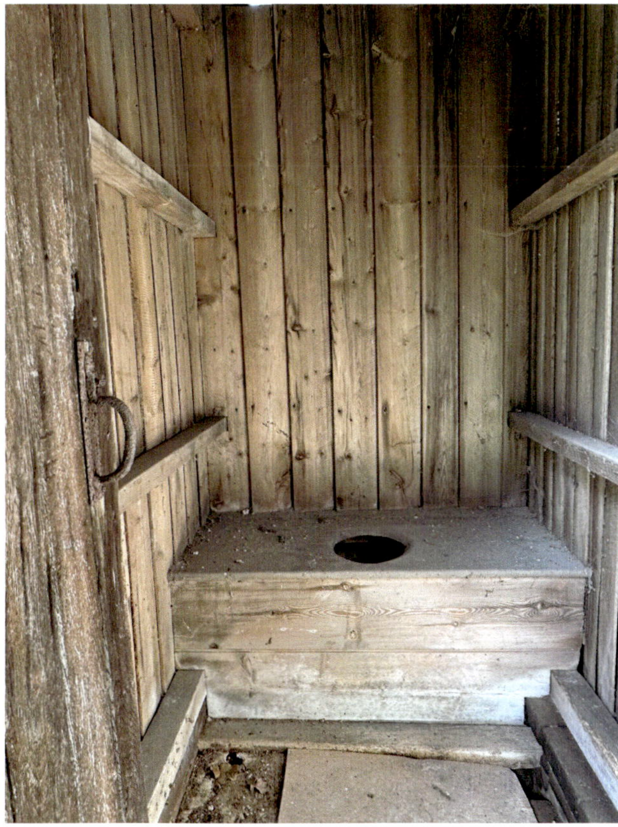

Pentlow. In the churchyard is a rare survival indeed – a nineteenth-century privy!

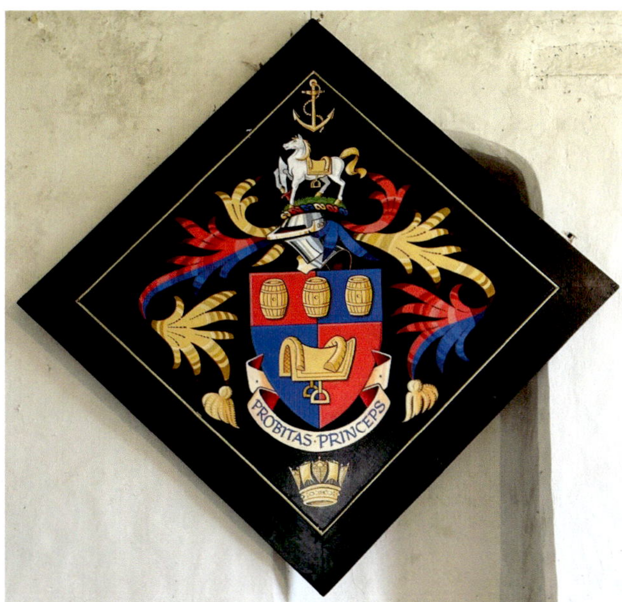

Pentlow. Funeral hatchments were popular in the seventeenth and eighteenth centuries, but this one dates from 2017 and remembers Clifford Stuchfield.

39. Purleigh, All Saints

The church stands in a wonderful location, high above its village with views to the estuary of the Blackwater. The churchyard contains the grave of Sergeant Adam Eves, a policeman who was murdered in 1893 when he approached four local men who were carrying wheat they had stolen from a local farm. There are also some fine eighteenth-century lozenge-shaped 'body stones' under the yew trees by the porch – a local speciality. The church is fourteenth century in date, but you enter via a Tudor brick porch which would have been known to the seventeenth-century rector, Lawrence Washington, ancestor of America's President George Washington. Unlike most churches, there is no change of floor level between nave and chancel, which here is empty, creating a light and useful space. The south arcade displays notches in the capitals to show that it was formerly divided by wooden screens. A window in the south aisle contains fragments of medieval glass made up into a St Cuthbert's Cross. Dominating the nave is an enormous late seventeenth-century pulpit reached via a grand staircase with barley twist balusters. At the east end the striking reredos, now sadly without its riddel curtains, depicts the Lamb of God and the 'noble army of martyrs'. Its Georgian predecessor is now split up at the back of the church. The Decalogue, Creed and Ten Commandments stand by the

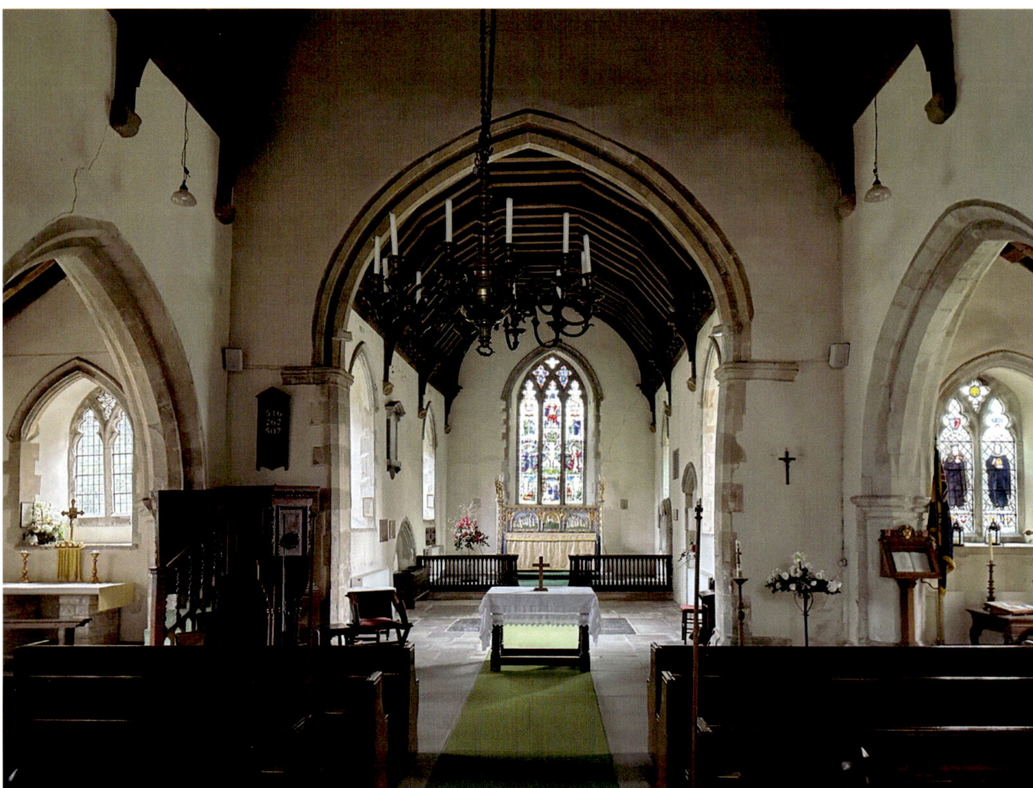

Purleigh. Interior looking east. Unusually, nave and chancel are on the same level. The pulpit is seventeenth century, the altar rails eighteenth century and the altar twentieth century.

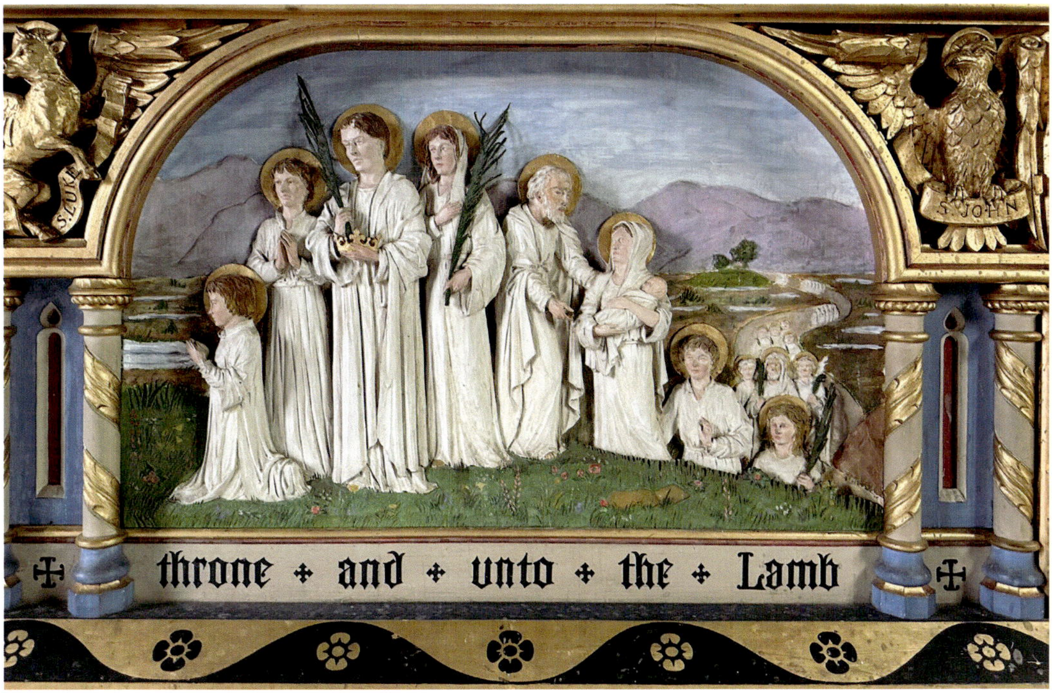

Purleigh. The reredos shows the 'noble army of martyrs' carrying the palm branch, the symbol of martyrdom. It dates from 1938 and was designed by Roger Hedley of Newcastle.

font whilst the paintings of Moses and Aaron that accompanied them are now on the west wall. In the north wall of the chancel is a plain fourteenth-century tomb recess which is now home to a large chest with the customary three locks for the rector and churchwardens. To the south of the altar stands a sedilia and (damaged) piscina. Nearby is a beautifully inscribed brass inscription to Cecilia (d. 1599) who was the widow of Bishop Edmund Freake. Other clerics commemorated in the church include John Wycliffe and John Keble. The former was a fourteenth-century priest whose work is often seen as a precursor to the Reformation, whilst the latter was to influence what became known as the Oxford Movement in the nineteenth century. The window was designed by A. K. Nicholson in 1932.

40. Rayleigh, Holy Trinity

Most medieval churches were built as 'community efforts', funded by numerous small donations, and only those few donors whose names were recorded at the time are known. Here at Rayleigh, the donors who paid for the piers in the south aisle in the fifteenth century had their names recorded on the parts to which they had contributed – a rare and pleasing discovery. Holy Trinity has recently been reordered and is a fine example of how to make a medieval building work in the twenty-first century. It is a very wide church for its length, best seen outside when viewed from the east with chapels to north and south of the chancel. The north chapel east window is curiously off-centre, although it is not as obvious from inside. When a church was consecrated, the bishop applied holy oil to twenty-four points inside and outside. At the west end of the nave two crosses painted on the wall survive to indicate the locations; the rest have been lost. At the east end of the north aisle the stairs to the rood loft survive, indicating the height of the screen which ran the full width of the church. Above the chancel arch is a wooden-framed opening that must have been associated with the rood itself, which was painted high on the east wall. The church contains three treasures. The first is a very early dug-out chest, probably thirteenth century and relatively small. It has just one lock so predates the time when three locks were stipulated. In the south chapel is an important Tudor monument erected by the Alleyn family. Sadly, devoid of its original bright colours, it is nonetheless still a decorative piece. At the base are quatrefoil panels which must have been painted with the Alleyn Shields of arms. Above it are five recesses designed to take statues, all covered by a panelled ceiling and parapet. It may have originally stood elsewhere in the church and been used as an Easter sepulchre as it has the traditional tabletop. The last of the treasures is to be found under the tower: a royal arms with the initials of Queen Anne (1702–1714). Interestingly, Anne had her own motto, '*Semper Eadem*', but this one has the more usual royal motto of '*Dieu et Mon Droit*'.

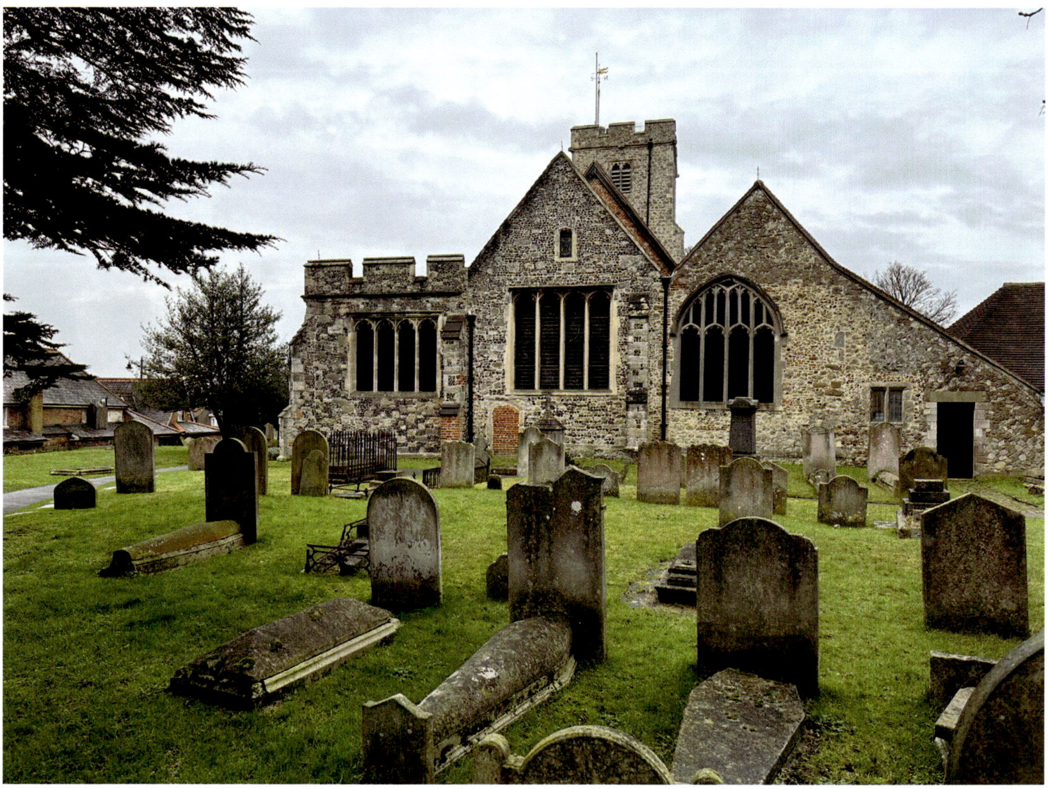

Rayleigh. Seen from the east we can identify the chancel with north and south chapels. The church is mainly of flint and ragstone. In the foreground are some Georgian 'bodystone' graves.

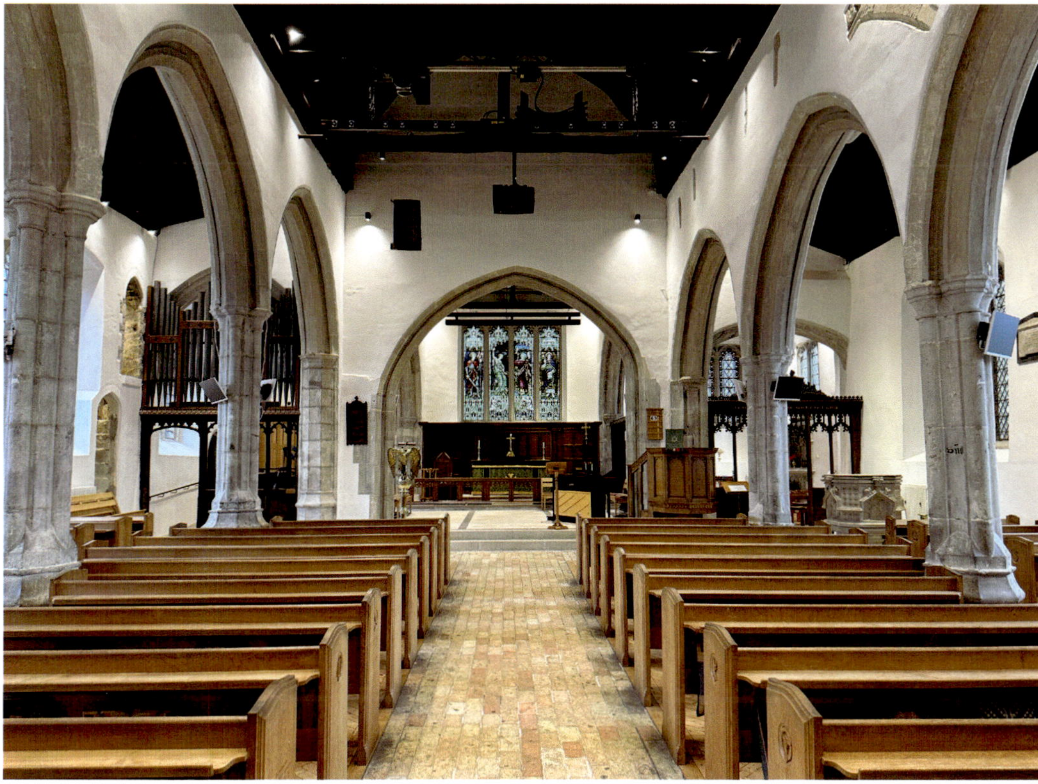

Rayleigh. The recently reordered interior. On the far left-hand side the rood loft stairs can be seen. As they are in an outer wall we know the screen ran the full width of the church.

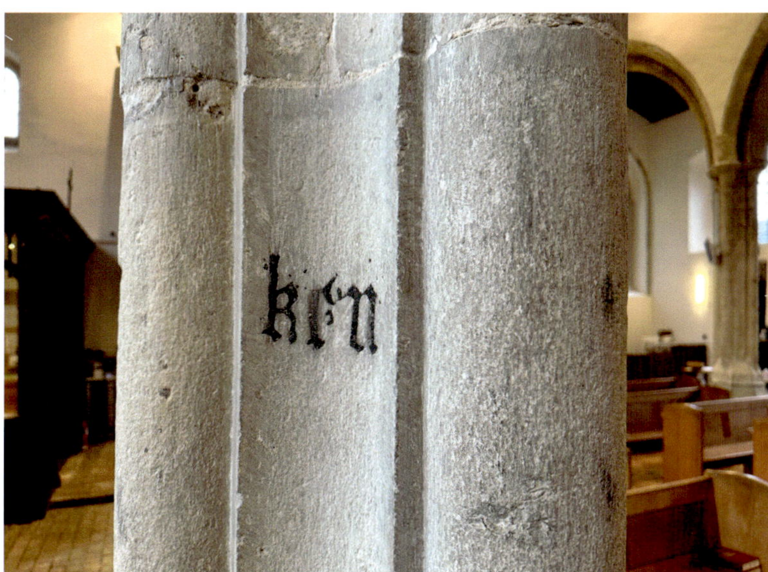

Rayleigh. The piers in the south aisle each carry the initials of the person who contributed to their construction. Medieval churches were often community builds.

It may be that these arms were introduced in the reign of Charles II or James II and Anne's initials added after her accession. In any case it dates from before the Act of Union of 1707 (see the same design at 18. Fingringhoe). Also under the tower is a carved beam with carved strapwork decoration which, it is said, supported a private gallery in the seventeenth century. Before you leave, don't miss the very moving carved Crucifixion scene in the south aisle which forms part of the First World War memorial. A wounded soldier lies on a battlefield scene looking up at Christ.

41. Stanford Rivers, St Margaret

For any building constructed of flint rubble, the major issue is damp. The large areas of mortar between the irregularly shaped stones allow rain to seep through and into the interior. The original builders recognised this and applied a thick lime render to the outside which helped, but later generations allowed it to fall off so that by the time the Victorians inherited our churches they were always in a poor state of repair. Their solution was to replace the render using their 'new' wonder material – cement. Today we regret their use of cement as it looks ugly and doesn't help the building at all, but we're stuck with it. As you walk down the avenue

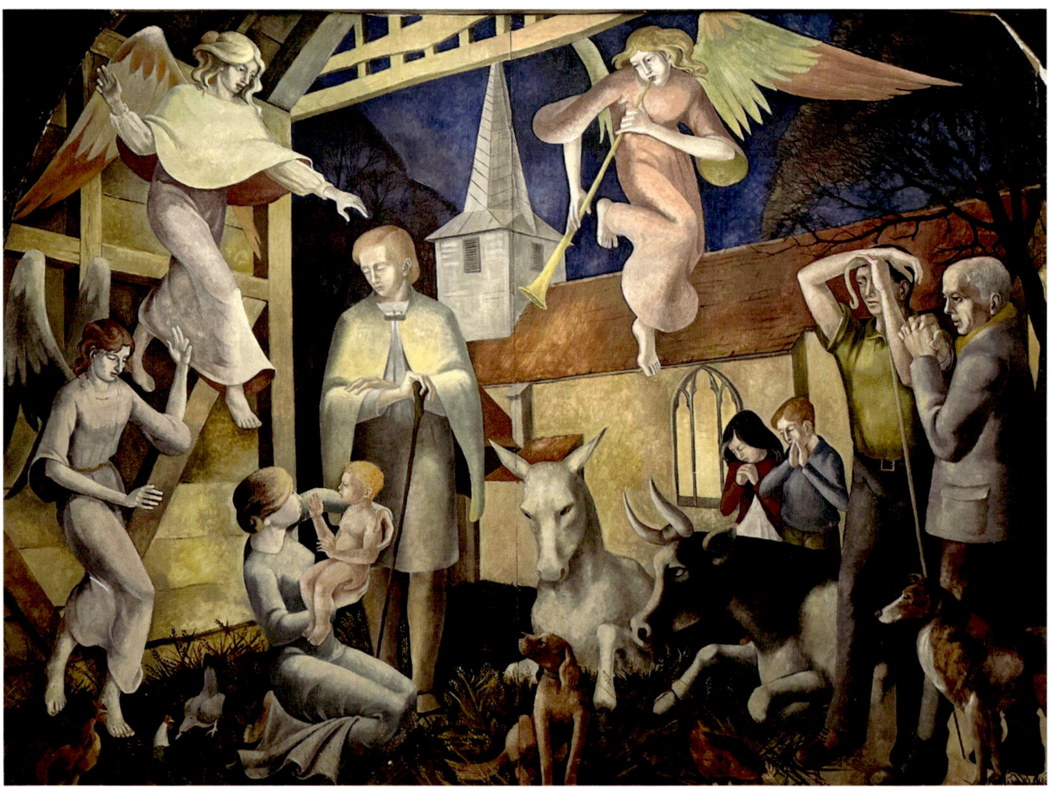

Stanford Rivers. Beneath the gallery is this depiction of the Nativity by Fyffe Christie painted in 1961. He incorporated the church into his design.

to St Margaret's you pass the grave of the composer Noel Gay, best known for the 'Lambeth Walk' and 'Run Rabbit, Run'. You enter the church under a west gallery which is partly made up with tracery from the medieval rood screen, and immediately see the feature for which the church is best known – a painting of the Nativity by Fyffe Christie (1918–1979), painted on boards in 1961. Christie is famous for his war paintings and for his work produced from the Glasgow School of Art. Here he sets the scene with Stanford church in the background. It's one of the most important twentieth-century artworks in an Essex church. The building itself is remarkably simple, with original Norman windows visible at the west end of the nave, the rest being replaced in later building campaigns. There is no chancel arch, which means the building seems much longer than usual. Two modern stained-glass windows incorporate much clear glass. The seating is interesting in that there are open benches for the poor at the rear and box pews at the front which would have been rented by the wealthier famers. The altar rails are made from heavy turned balusters and enclose a sanctuary rich in monuments. In front of the altar are a series of black ledgerstones to the Petre family, but there are also some important medieval memorial brasses too. Thomas Greville, son of a London merchant, is shown in his swaddling clothes having died 'in his tender age' in 1492. It is an early use of English, as opposed to Latin, on a memorial. Nearby, the early sixteenth-century brass to Robert and Alice Borrow has, at Robert's feet, a little dog looking loyally up to his master. On the north wall is a less impressive, but no less important, brass to Thomas Green, who died in 1535. Unusually, it records the frequency that a priest was to pray for his soul, his wives, children and all Christian souls.

42. Stansted Mountfitchet, St Mary

A long walk from the famous Norman motte-and-bailey castle and village, St Mary's is well worth the journey, displaying high-quality features from the last 900 years. It may look a little clinical from outside as the tower is eighteenth-century brick and the rest of the church comprehensively rebuilt by the Victorians, but it's the inside that draws the visitor. It doesn't matter if you enter the north or south doors because both of them represent the best Romanesque architecture in Essex, with zig-zag mouldings and three orders of arches. Once inside you'll see that the chancel arch is of the same period, but it's not set centrally in the east wall so as part of the Victorian rebuilding Thomas Dollman brought the roof on the south side in on a series of brackets to make the interior appear more symmetrical. In the north chapel is the rather battered effigy (*c*. 1300) of a member of the Lancaster family. In the north aisle is the famous painted alabaster monument to Hester Salusbury, who died in 1614. The pieces of sculpture on the wall above were once part of the monument and represent symbols of the Passion, a rare thing to find at this period. Hester's father, Thomas Myddleton (d. 1631) is commemorated by the huge monument by the altar. It depicts a sarcophagus at the bottom with straps held in place by skulls. Then a praying effigy of the deceased, followed by a lengthy inscription all surrounded by much heraldry and figures of virtues. The church contains some very interesting stained glass. The jewel-like east window of the Lancaster Chapel, which depicts the Good Samaritan, is signed in a tiny shield by William Warrington,

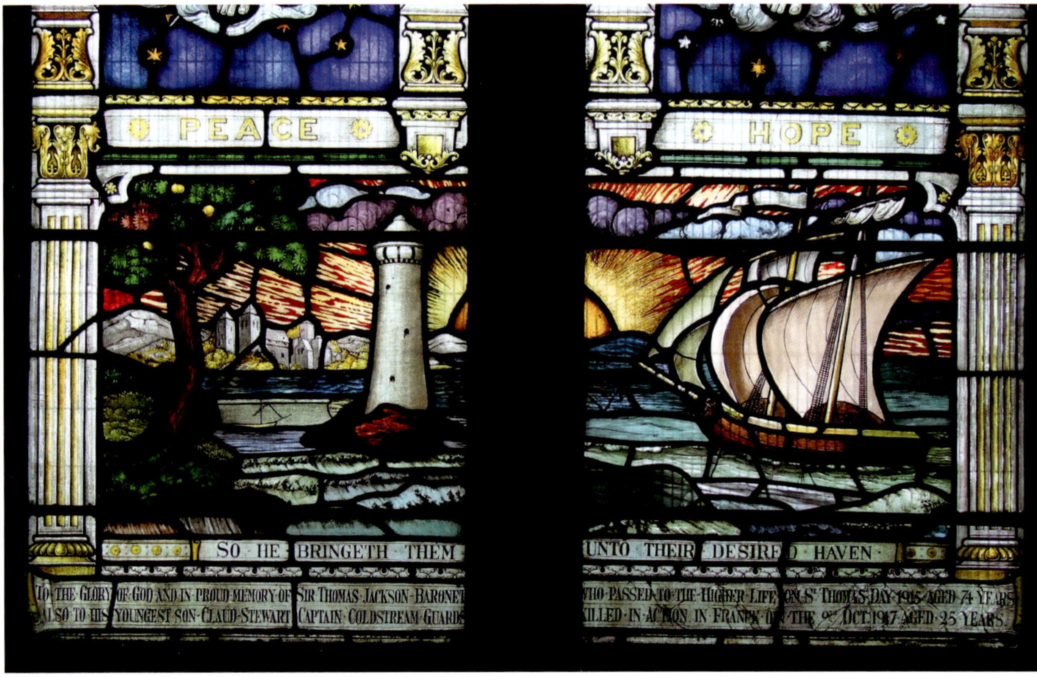

Stansted Mountfitchet. This stained-glass window depicting a ship coming safely into harbour was designed by Clayton and Bell as a memorial to a chief manager of HSBC.

1859. The west window depicts two angels as Peace and Hope and shows a ship (representing the Soul) safely entering a harbour with a lighthouse. It is a memorial by the firm of Clayton and Bell to Sir Thomas Jackson (d. 1915), Chief Manager of HSBC. An elaborate brass panel records the death of Robert-Fuller Maitland, who was killed by an elephant whilst big-game hunting in East Africa in 1887. The Fuller-Maitlands owned Stansted Hall, which can be glimpsed from the churchyard, through the late nineteenth and early twentieth centuries.

43. Thaxted, St John the Baptist

One of the showpiece churches of Essex, built out of the proceeds of the wool trade and prominently sited on the top of the hill in this charming small town. It dates from the late medieval period, when the town was at its wealthiest – a period of 200 years from about 1350. When the large windows were filled with stained glass it must have been a wonderful sight, although today's clear glass creates an equally impressive interior. In fact, large amounts of medieval glass survive in fragmentary form and a pair of binoculars will allow the details to be studied. My favourite detail is of a watermill in the north chapel. Dividing the aisles are screens which have lost their tracery, but the surviving dados are full of carved details with bats, dragons, birds and monsters. At the west end is a most unusual font cover which encases the font from the floor upwards, the middle section opening to allow baptism to be performed. It dates from the fifteenth century – a time

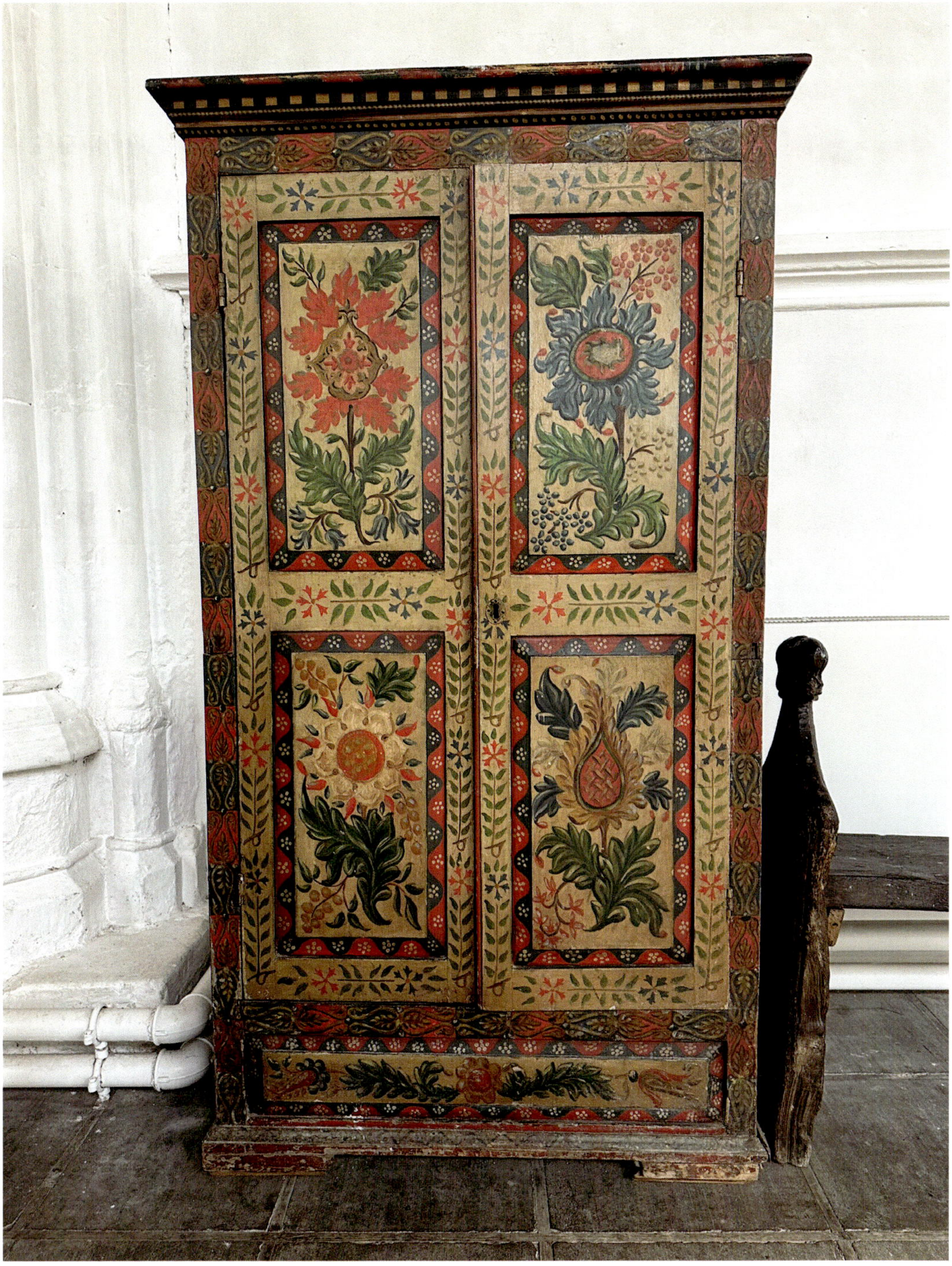

Thaxted. In the early twentieth century this cupboard was upcycled by the eccentric Marquis d'Oisy to make it more acceptable in the eyes of God.

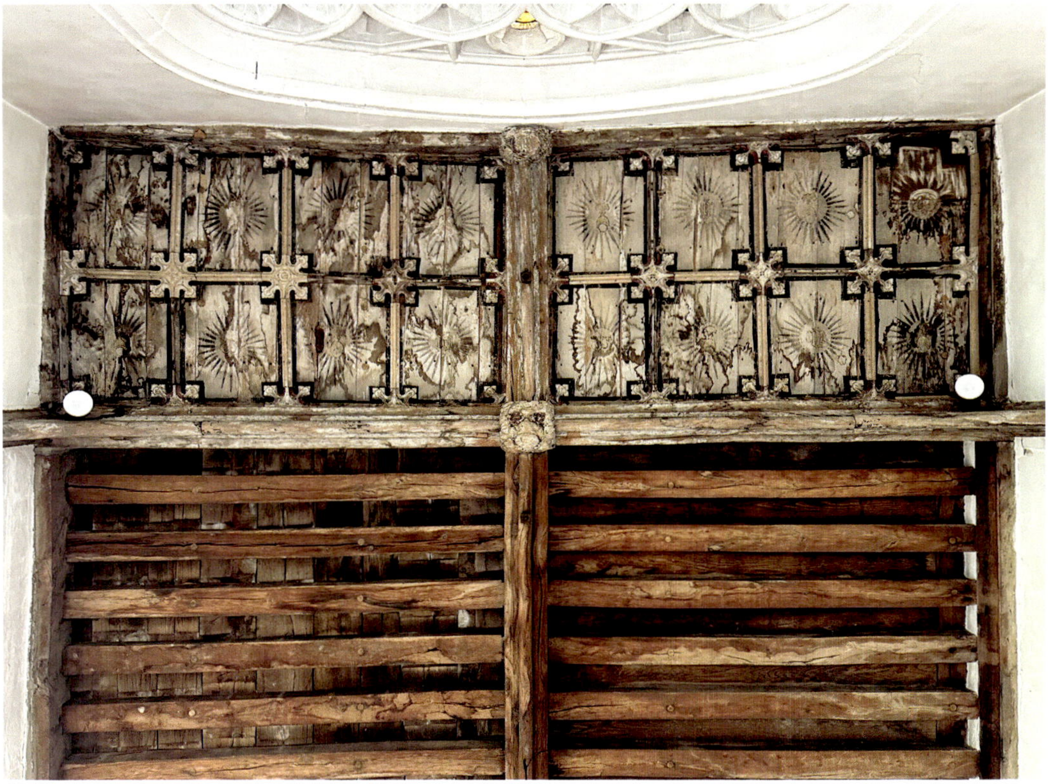

Thaxted. This painted ceiling with images of a chalice set within a sunburst and the sacred IHS monogram is known as a celure and was painted to give honour to the altar beneath.

before we used screws, so the hinges are solidly nailed in place! The enormous royal coat of arms cutout in wood are those of Queen Anne, and on the opposite wall of the south aisle are fragmentary remains of wall paintings. The roof here is of particular interest, with superb wooden bosses. The visitor will notice that there are few monuments in the church. It is likely that its original benefactors were buried in prestigious locations in nearby monasteries (see 44. Tilty) and that in subsequent periods the majority of parishioners were impoverished, the large Georgian houses being second homes for families whose main houses were in the City. For thirty years in the early twentieth century the incumbent here was Revd Conrad Noel (d. 1942). He is commemorated by a bronze bust by Gertrude Hermes. Noel was given the job by Daisy, Countess of Warwick (see 44. Tilty) and shared her progressive socialist views, going so far as to display the Red Flag and that of Sinn Féin in the church until ordered to desist. He was an Anglo-Catholic and the church still reflects his influence today. One of his friends was the Marquis d'Oisy, a failed postulant who was ahead of his time in being an 'up-cycler'. The church contains some examples of his work, including his generous repainting of a cupboard and the decoration of the wooden lectern. Earlier woodwork in the church includes a painted celure, or canopy, giving honour to an altar.

44. Tilty, St Mary the Virgin

The Cistercians were one of the many monastic orders to split away from the Benedictine way of life, feeling that a more austere lifestyle would better suit their beliefs. Their monasteries were always in out of the way places where they wouldn't be disturbed. The way in which their houses were planned differed from all other communities in that they always had a separate chapel for visitors to use, normally freestanding and situated outside the gate. We now know these as a capella ante portas. And this is what survives at Tilty, later converted to a parish church. It is a simple building but one of great charm. The huge east window takes up almost the entire east wall of the fourteenth-century chancel which was an addition to the original thirteenth-century building. From the outside it is easy to see this as an addition as it is much taller and has its own roof structure. It alone has visible flint walling, for the nave is completely rendered in an ochre lime plaster. On the south side there are four Early English lancet windows, but

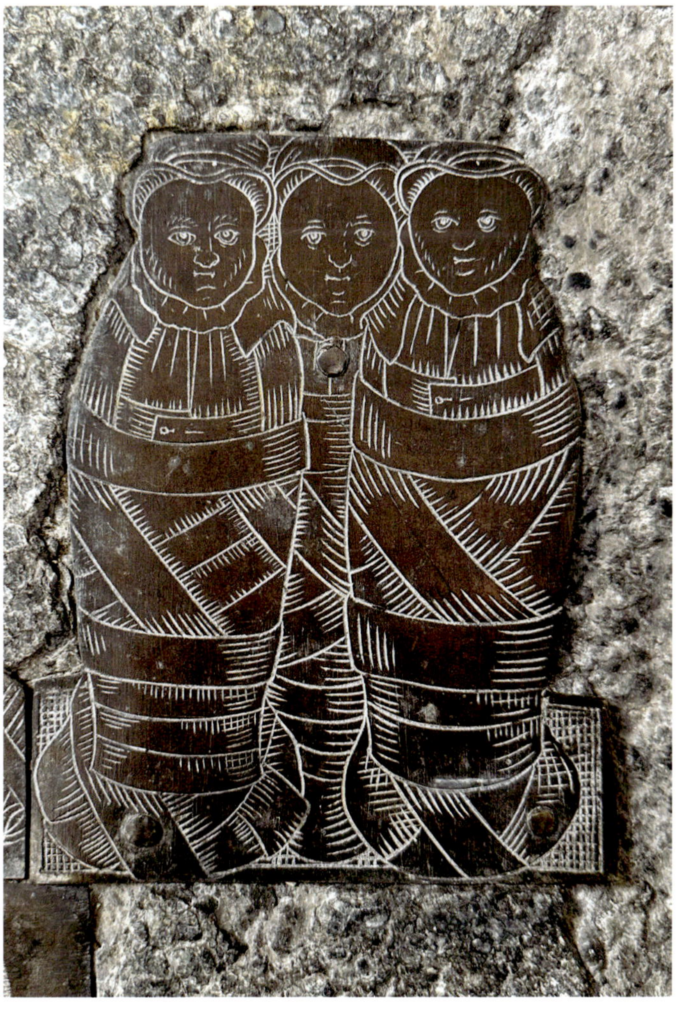

Tilty. Three babies in swaddling appear on the Tuke memorial brass dating from 1590.

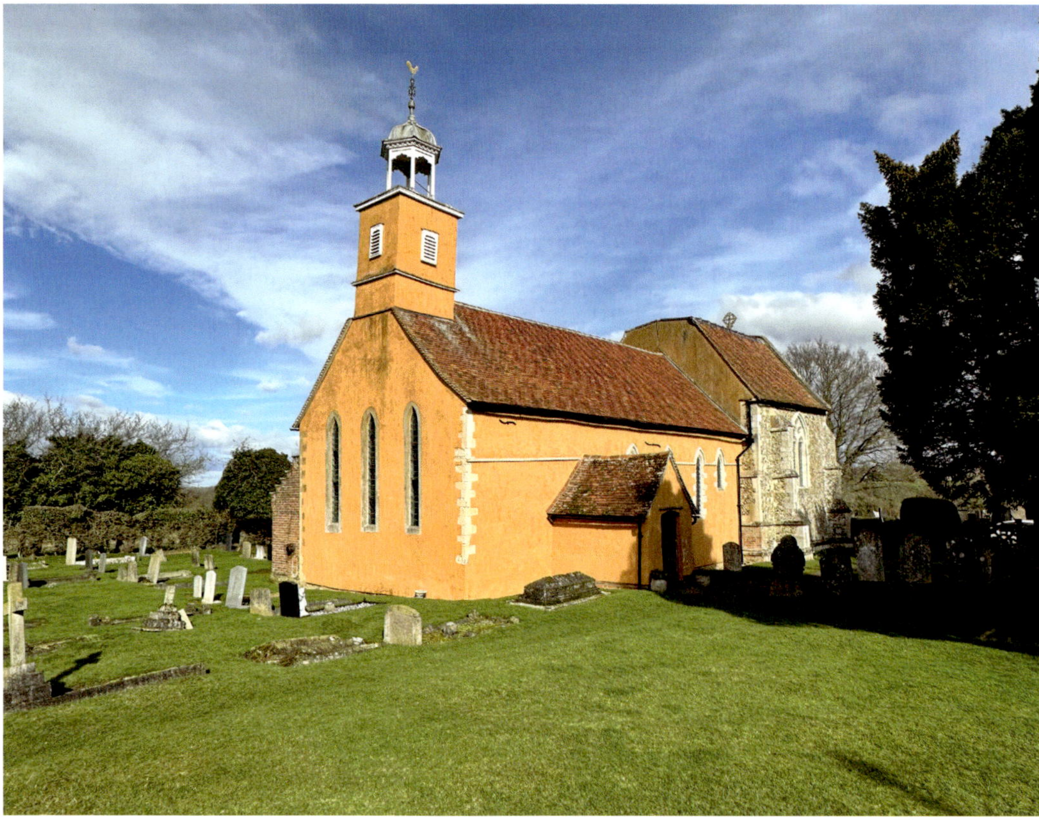

Tilty. Exterior from the south-west showing the thirteenth-century nave of the *Capella ante Portus* of the Cistercian abbey. The chancel to the right was a fourteenth-century addition.

the easternmost is shorter than the others to give space below for a sedilia, which became redundant when the new chancel was added on. Inside everything is light and it is easy to spot the things of special interest. A wooden heraldic monument hangs in the nave, similar to the one at East Mersea (see entry 16), although the inscription is barely readable. The hatchment above is a fine representation of the Maynard shield of arms, underneath a viscount's coronet and with a stag and talbot as supporters. On the north wall of the chancel are the bottoms of two stone coffins (complete with drain holes and runnels) which were excavated from the main abbey. In the floor is a tomb slab incised with a large standing cross and a Lombardic inscription around the edge. These inscriptions would originally have been filled with pitch (see 12. Corringham). Within the sanctuary are some sixteenth-century brasses. That to Margaret Tuke (d. 1590) shows her three sons, two daughters and three babies in swaddling. Tilty church underwent considerable refurbishment in the twentieth century at which time the eccentric Marquis d'Oisy painted the font cover and the underside of the sounding board over the pulpit. These discrete splashes of colour work very well in an otherwise white interior.

45. WALTHAM ABBEY, HOLY CROSS AND ST LAWRENCE

Essex had a large number of monastic foundations, several of which have survived as today's parish churches. At Waltham the impressive parish church is less than a quarter of the size it once was, representing just the nave of the Romanesque foundation, but what a fragment it is. The church is entered under a sixteenth-century west tower where, high above your head, is an excellent example of the royal arms of King Charles II. The church dates in the main from the twelfth century with its solid piers, semicircular arches, triforium and clerestory, although it is apparent that this is not a single design but several different campaigns, as new masons were appointed with slightly different ideas. The east wall is nineteenth century, filling the gap where the building would have continued to the east. It was built by William Burges, who did much work of high quality here including the altar and reredos. But the highlight of his work for most visitors is the painted wooden ceiling, which illustrates the Signs of the Zodiac and the Labours of the Months. A mirror is provided to help the visitor appreciate it. You'll notice that the ceiling is constructed of wooden planks but that the painted panels are of canvas so that the joins don't interfere with the designs. To the south of the church is a Guild Chapel built in the fourteenth century and now containing

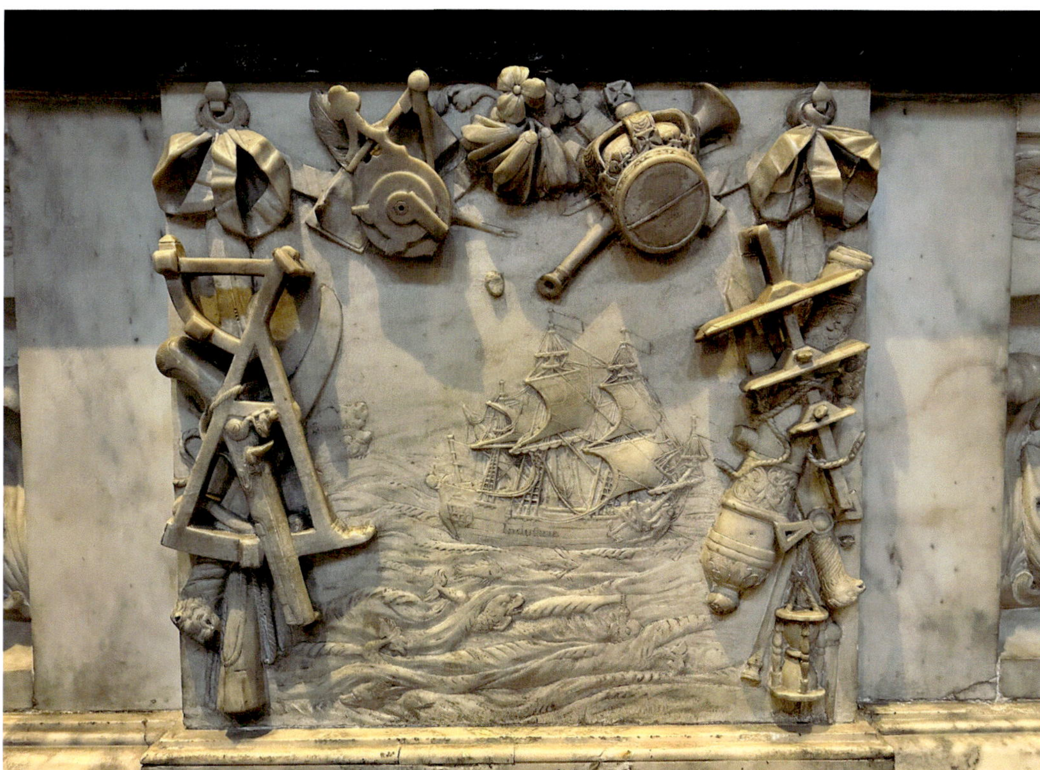

Waltham Abbey. This detail from the monument to Robert Smith shows a ship called *Industria* surrounded by objects associated with foreign travel.

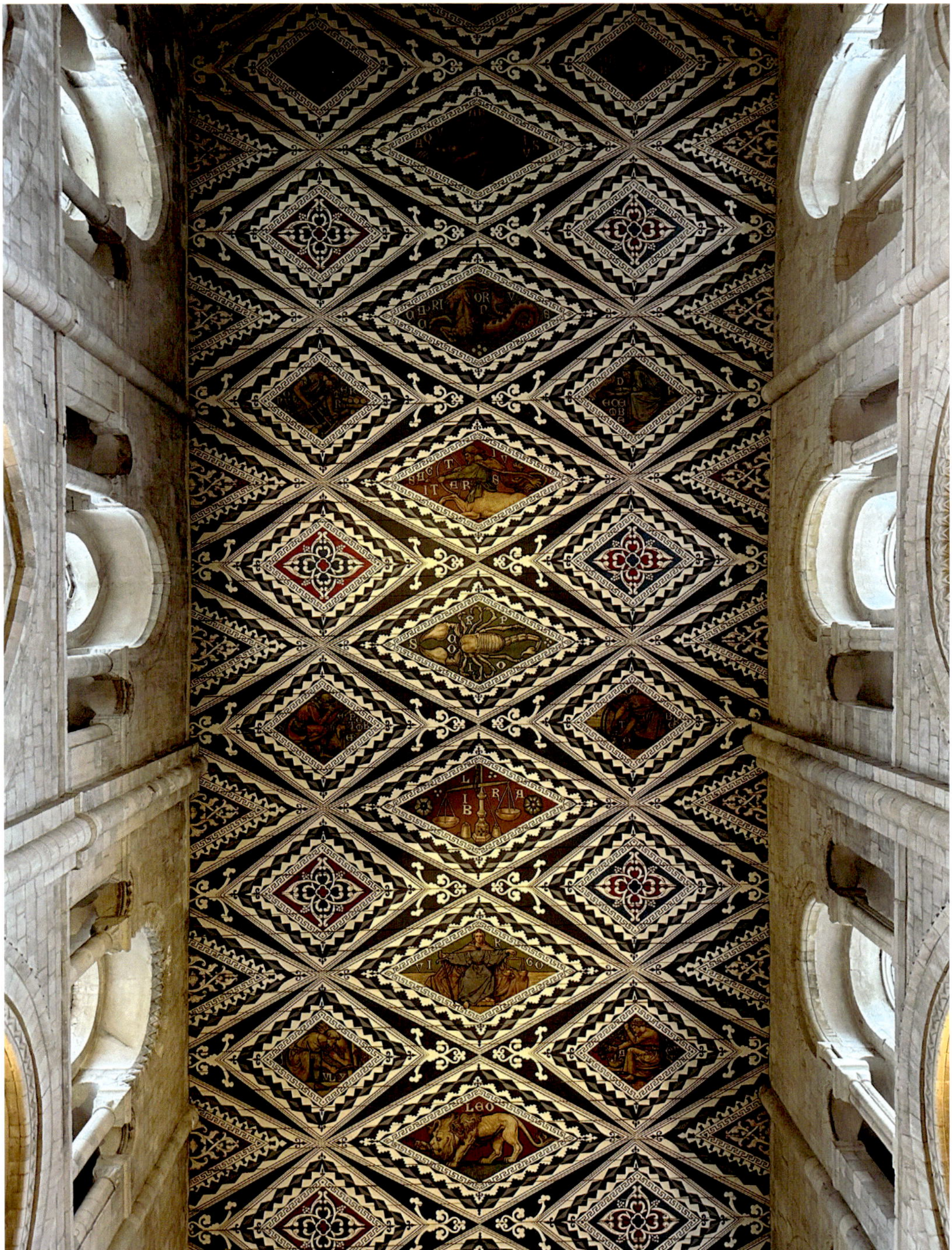

Waltham Abbey. The painting on the nave roof, designed by William Burges, depicts the Signs of the Zodiac and the Labours of the Months.

the gift shop. Its east wall has a large painting of the Doom, with the dead being raised on the left-hand side and the damned heading towards the Jaws of Hell on the right. There are several fine monuments to discover. Near the chapel is the early seventeenth-century painted monument to Sir Edward Denny, his wife and their myriad children (including a blind son) underneath. It was his ancestor who demolished the greater part of the building following the Dissolution of the Monasteries. In the north aisle is a late seventeenth-century memorial to Robert Smith which depicts a ship named *Industria* surrounded by fantastic carvings of cannon, an hourglass, dividers, a crown compass and a cutlass. All objects familiar to Smith who travelled the world and who, the inscription records, 'brought back fame and riches'. Nearby, and almost unnoticed amongst the showstopping architecture is a simple fourteenth-century wooden screen with peep holes in its base to allow people kneeling in the aisle to have a view of an altar the other side.

46. Wendens Ambo, St Mary the Virgin

A much-photographed church which, despite its proximity to large conurbations, still presents as the much-loved heart of a rural community. It has its origins in a Norman tower which reuses Roman brick both in its structure and also as the surround for the west doorway. Topping it off is a 'Hertfordshire Spike', a feature of churches further west but sometimes found just into Essex. On the south side the porch has a roof structure taller than the nave to which it joins – it was rebuilt by Fr Ernest Geldart (see 32. Little Braxted). The walls of the nave

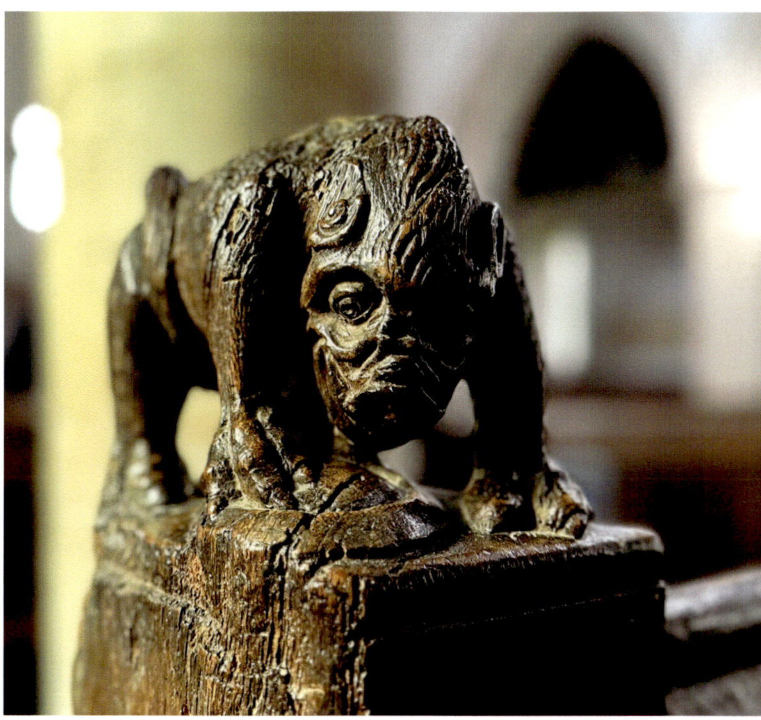

Wendens Ambo. On the end of this medieval bench is a carving of a tiger looking down into a mirror and thinking it is seeing its cub.

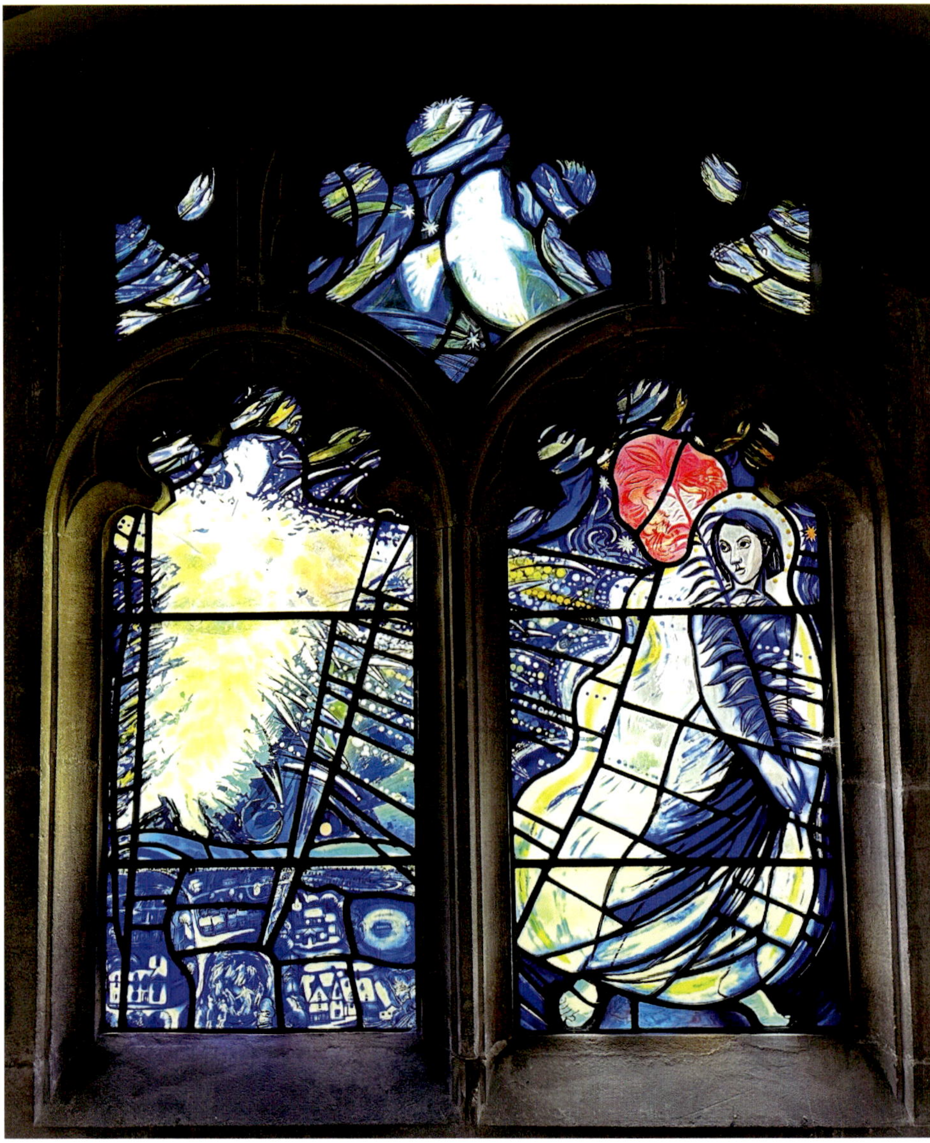

Wendens Ambo. The Annunciation in stained glass designed by Peter Caller in 2002. In the bottom left-hand corner you can see the village complete with church.

were raised in the fifteenth century to introduce a clerestory, but one window is of brick rather than stone. I wonder if they ran out of money? The south door leads us into a church where we can compare the round-piered thirteenth-century south arcade with the octagonal piers of the fourteenth-century north aisle. Opposite the door is a stunning window installed in 2002 by Peter Caller depicting the Annunciation. The archangel is shown as almost a featureless shape at whose feet the village of Wendens Ambo is shown, whilst Mary doesn't know which way to turn. In the chancel we can find some fragments of medieval English glass together with some Netherlandish roundels of the sixteenth century. Look for St Mark writing his Gospel with his bored lion as a companion! The prettily painted eighteenth-century organ was built for a domestic setting and was brought here in the nineteenth century when Fr Geldart designed an organ chamber especially for it. In the south aisle are two items not to be missed. The first is a large memorial brass to William Loveney which dates from the early years of the fifteenth century. He is now mounted on the wall to save further deterioration. Next to him is the most famous thing people come to see. It is the sole surviving medieval bench end in the church and represents a tiger looking into a convex mirror. This is from a thirteenth-century legend that says if you want to steal a tiger cub you need to put a mirror down so that when the mother tiger looks into it she thinks she is looking at her cub and doesn't notice that you've taken it away. Once a common image to be found in churches, only a few survive countrywide. Mind you, the carver of this one had probably only 'heard' what a tiger looked like!

47. West Bergholt, St Mary

This 'retired' church stands in an idyllic spot away from the village next to the Georgian hall. A walk around the outside shows the Saxon origins of the church with a prominent blocked north doorway, although most of the church dates from the thirteenth and fourteenth centuries. Look at the south door, its medieval woodwork pitted with hundreds of rusty nail holes showing how it has been used for centuries for displaying public notices. The interior is pleasantly unrestored, the uneven brick floors and plastered ceilings reminding us of the days before the Victorians drastically altered our churches in the pursuit of perfection. In the south aisle floor is the remains of a medieval stone coffin base with drain holes. The back of the church is dominated by a Georgian west gallery which contains bench seating for the poor. At a time when seats were rented you paid more for a solid back, whilst you rented open-backed benches for your servants who accompanied you to church. Gentlemen wore hats which were provided with their own pegs along the walls both in the gallery and downstairs. The front of the gallery displays a royal arms made in Colchester of cast iron in 1816 – it is one of twenty-three identical examples to be found in East Anglia. An earlier royal arms is painted on the wall high above the junction of nave and chancel. It dates from the reign of King James I and carries the motto 'Let God arise and let his enemies be scattered' from Psalm 68. The chancel floor shows ledgerstones over the graves of Mary Pollard and Rebecka Sadler who died within weeks of each other in 1676, suggesting they fell victim to the same illness, smallpox or plague. The interior is very light, helped by the magnificent east window by F. C. Eden (1928) which is set against a clear background. If you venture into the vestry under the gallery and look up, you will see a forest of timbers supporting the bell turret. These are of several different dates, cobbled together as subsequent churchwardens saw fit to support the bell. Nearby is the huge fifteenth-century chest with iron straps and protective nails to stop it being hacked open.

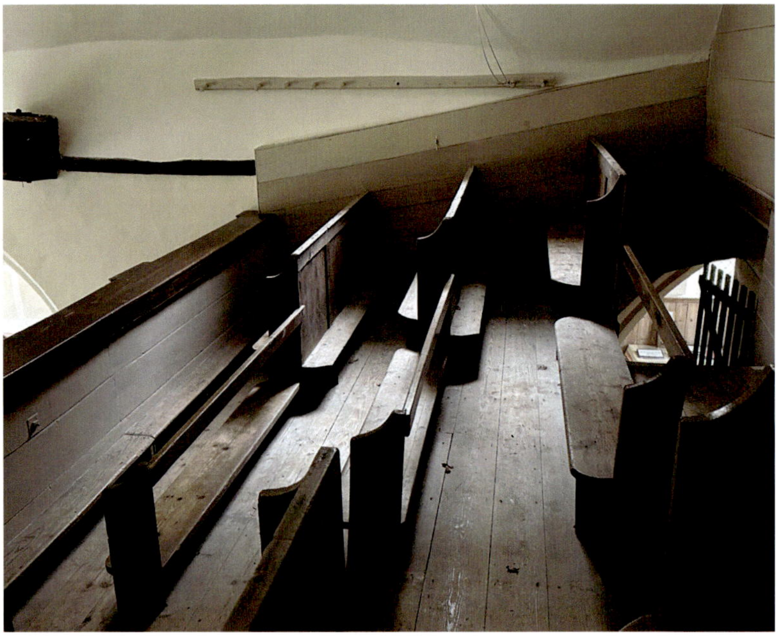

Left: West Bergholt. The gallery seating represents the social divisions in Georgian society with both backed and backless rented seats. Notice the hat pegs on the wall above.

Below: West Bergholt. The interior was re-seated by the Victorians, who removed the box pews. The painted royal arms are those of King James I.

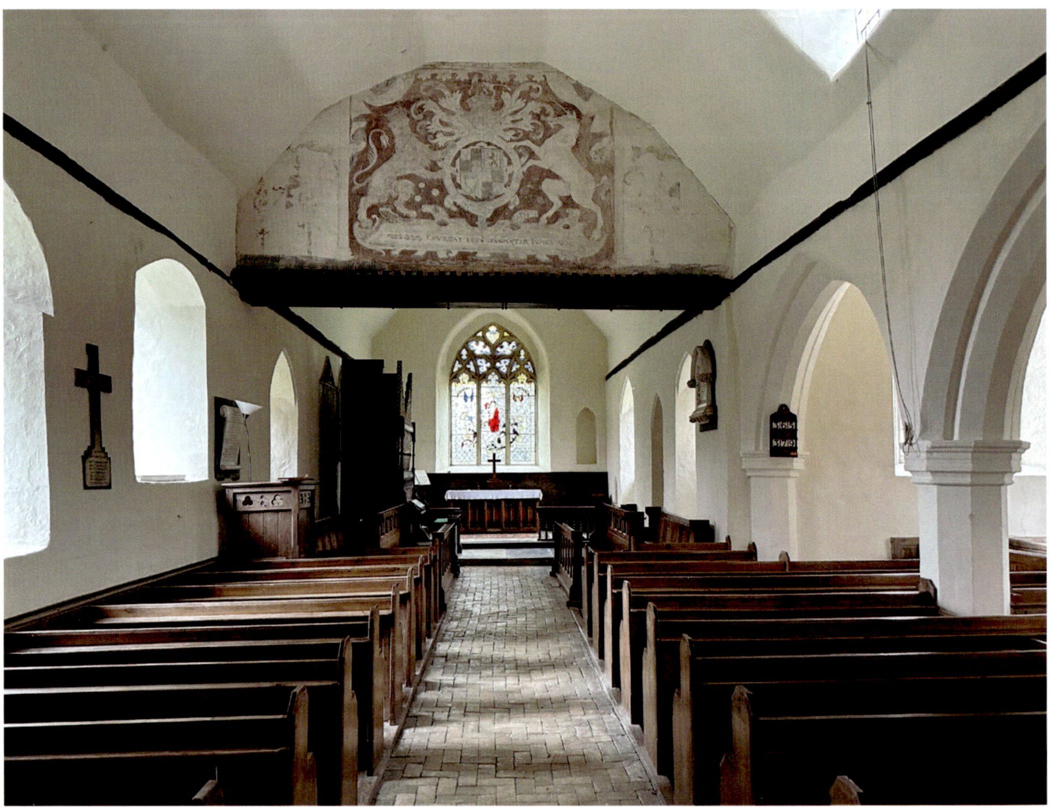

48. WETHERSFIELD, ST MARY MAGDALEN

The centre of Wethersfield is a delight, set around a sloping triangular green with the church peeping over the rooftops. Like many local churches, it is of flint origin with brick alterations. The base of the tower is open to the church and you can see how the structure is supported on a central vertical post. The south aisle, with its massive circular piers, dates from the thirteenth century and contrasts nicely with the north aisle where the octagonal piers are 100 years later. There are two windows by the French firm of Champigneulle: a crucifixion scene in the east window and a rather grislier memorial window to Everard Marsh, who was killed in 1880 during the Battle of Kandahar in Afghanistan, which shows him lying dead. Nearby are the more peaceful alabaster effigies of Sir Roger and Lady Wentworth (d. 1539) whose every flat surface has succumbed to the graffiti of successive generations. In the south aisle are some remarkable fragments of late medieval glass which include the crowned white falcon of Anne Boleyn, a boss-eyed lion and an ostrich holding a horseshoe in its beak. It was formerly believed that an ostrich could digest anything which is why it is often shown in this manner. In East Anglia it is the emblem of the earls of Leicester.

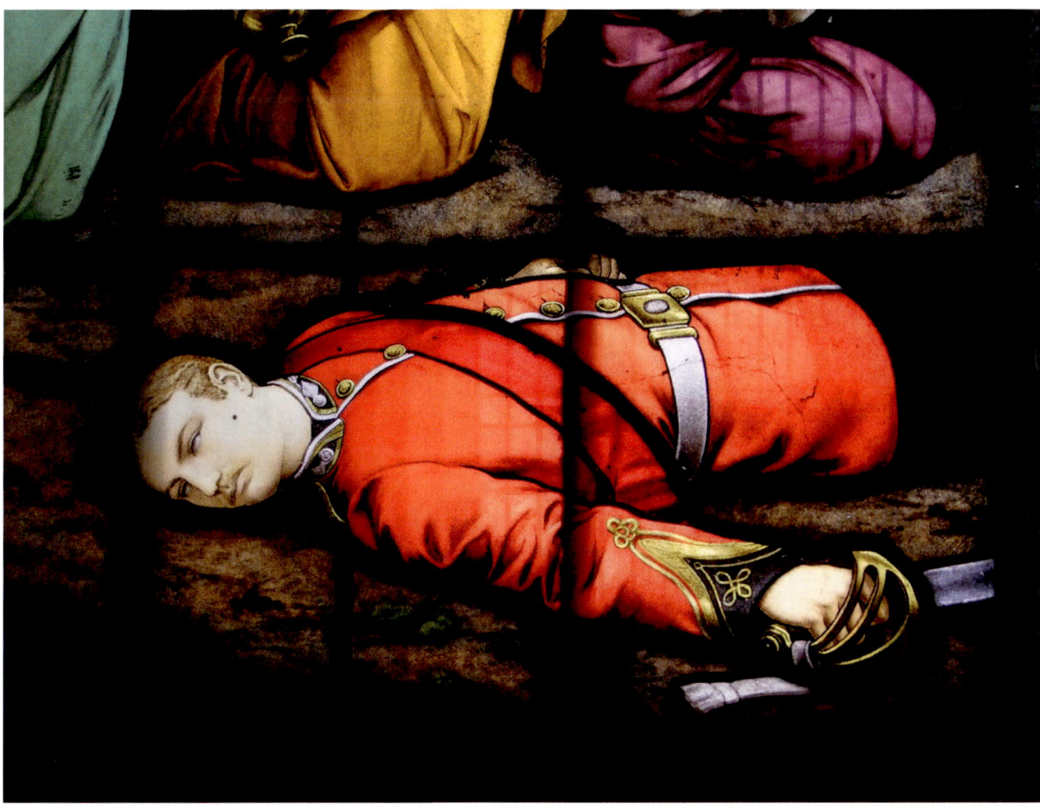

Wethersfield. This rather gruesome detail shows the dead Everard Marsh killed at the Battle of Kandahar in 1880. It was designed by the French firm of Champigneulle.

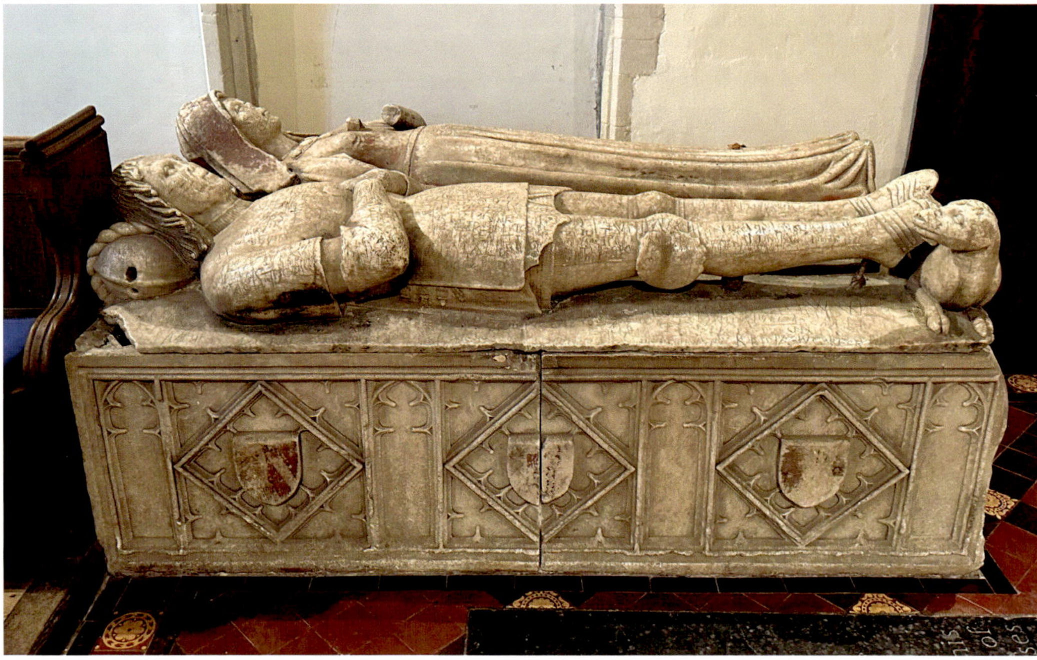

Wethersfield. Alabaster tomb of Sir Roger and Lady Wentworth, erected in the sixteenth century and covered with graffiti left by locals and travellers. Original paintwork remains.

49. Willingale Spain, St Andrew

At Willingale, two churches stand in a single churchyard, representing separate parishes whose boundaries met at this point. Remarkably, they were administered independently until 1929. The suffix of Spain is derived from the de Hispania family, the Norman lords of this manor. St Andrew's Church stands on the south side of the joint churchyard and consists of a nave and chancel of Norman origin. The outstanding feature of the interior is the metalwork of the north door which dates from the original church, although the door itself has been replaced. The huge iron hinges with their 'C' shape and ribbons of foliage are typical of this early date. You may need a torch to see it in detail as the back of the church can be very dark. Another early feature is the altar slab, or Mensa, which the Victorians reused on a modern frame. It is incised with five crosses to represent the five wounds of Christ. Its installation was achieved by Revd Ernest Geldart who also made the wooden cover for the font at the back of the church. The royal arms, recently conserved, are those of King George II (1727–60). They are very flamboyant and the supporters – the lion with his almost human face and the unicorn with his golden mane – are particularly lively. The quarters of the shield depict the territories he ruled, apart from the fleur-de-lys symbol, representing an ancient claim to the throne of France: the three lions of England are in the first quarter, the red lion of Scotland in the third and the harp of Ireland, and in the fourth are symbols of his German Dominions, including the white horse of Hanover. The church boasts much graffiti scratched into its dressed stonework over the centuries. A lot was added in the Second World War by US airman stationed nearby, but much earlier examples can be picked out, including two magnificent incised depictions of bishops on the south wall of the chancel.

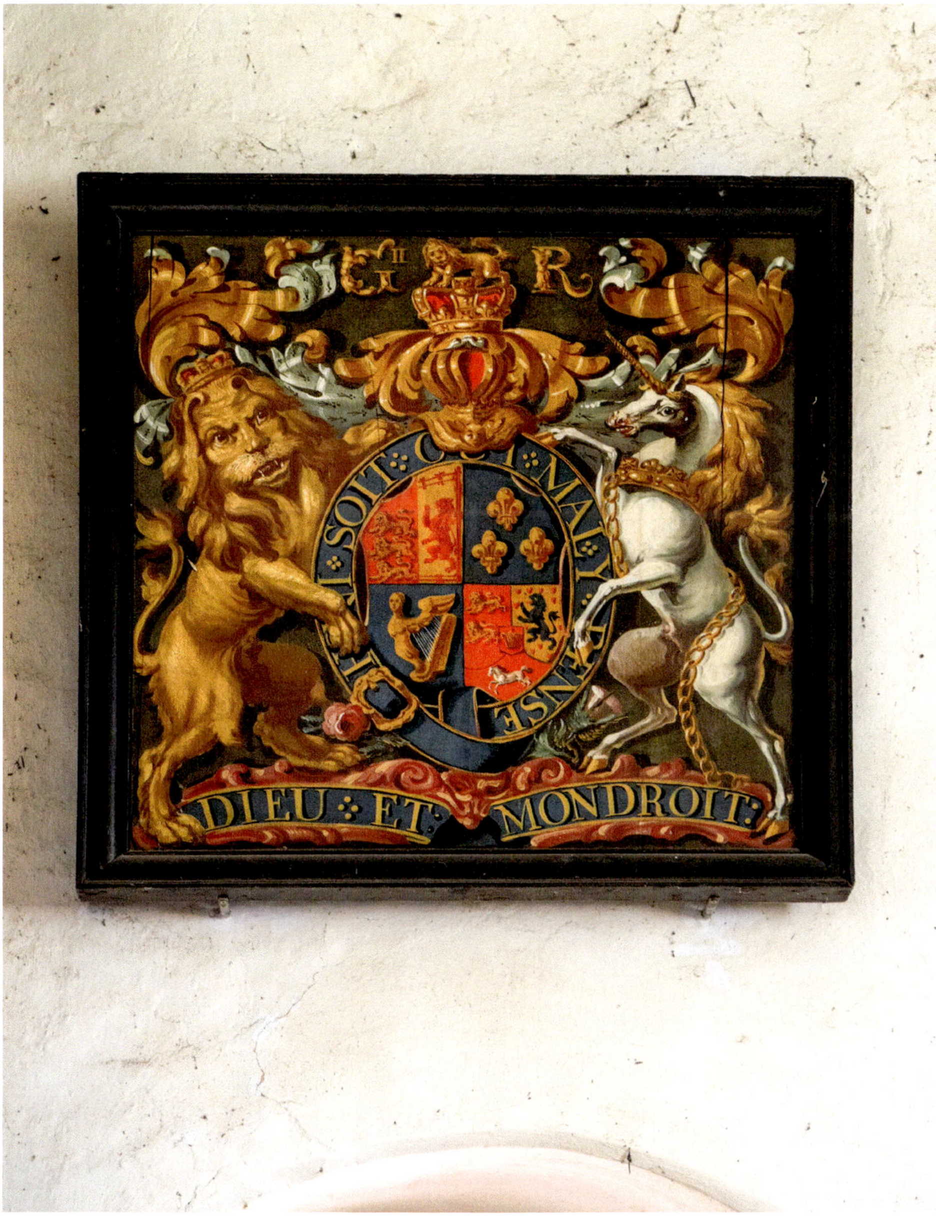

Willingale Spain. The royal arms, recently conserved, are those of King George II. At the time every Anglican church had by law to display a set. (Image by Adrian Powter)

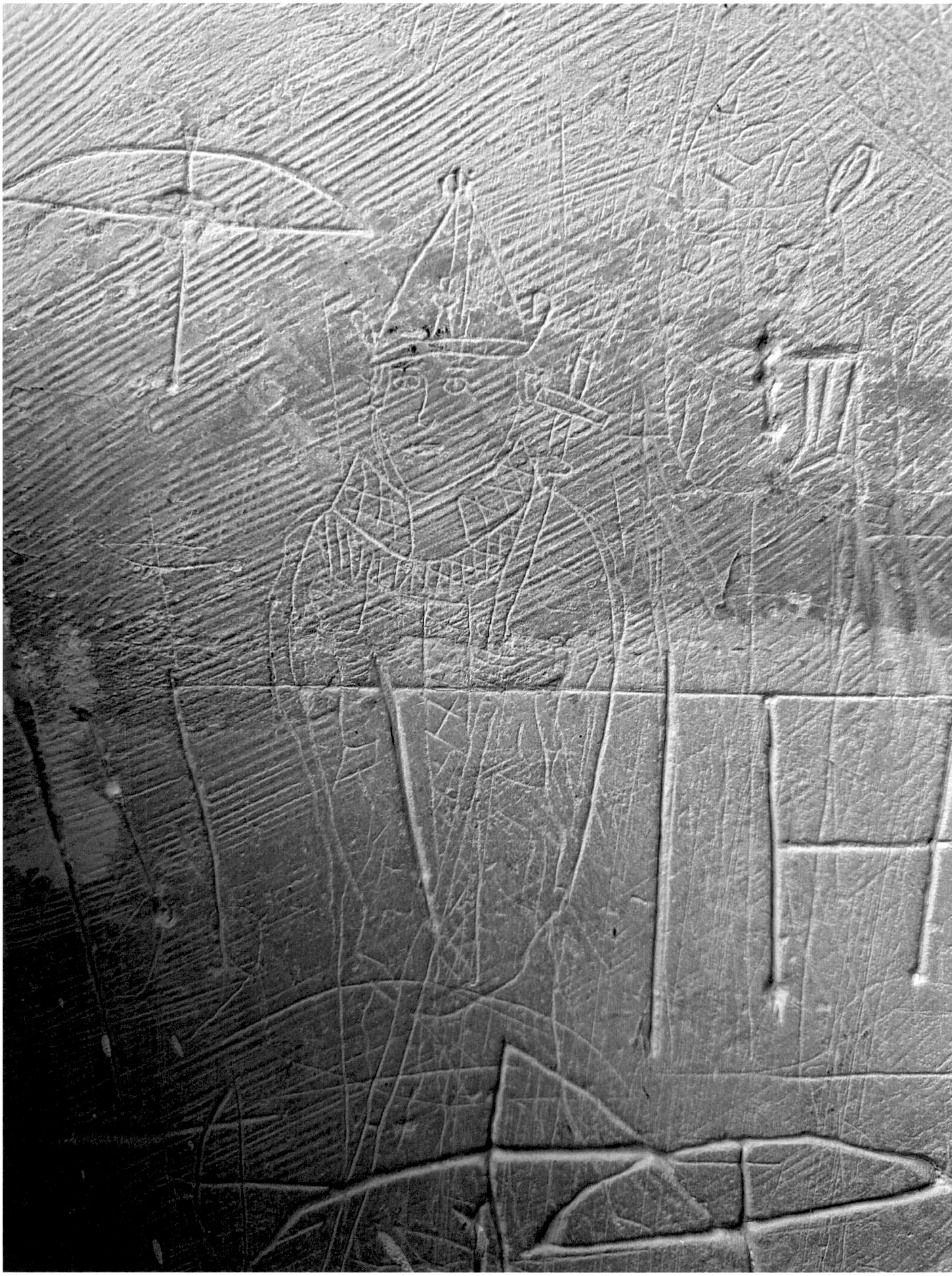

Willingale Spain. This medieval graffiti depicting a bishop is one of two to be found in this tiny church, but it takes a keen eye to find.